DATE DUE

Theodore Dreiser
A Checklist

Theodore Dreiser

A Checklist

By Hugh C. Atkinson
The Ohio State University

The Kent State University Press

The Serif Series
Bibliographies and Checklists, Number 15
William White, General Editor
Wayne State University

To Mary Rose

To Mary Rose

Preface

The checklist is meant to serve as a guide for the student, rather than as a definitive listing. Since the bibliographic work on Dreiser is so sparse, this checklist will, it is believed, be of some use to the serious scholar as well as to the student. This checklist is not complete, nor is it possible to make it so. A descriptive bibliography of the works of Dreiser is in preparation at the University of Pennsylvania. Many periodical appearances of Dreiser have yet to be discovered, especially those from the later years, and even more specifically those appearing in the left-wing ephemeral and occasional publications as well as the items in the *Daily* and in the *Sunday Worker*. The compiler hopes that additions and corrections to the checklist will be published in the appropriate journals by any who discover them. A checklist of this sort is built upon the work of others; acknowledgement of the work of Vrest Orton, Edward D. MacDonald, and Alfred Kazin and Charles Shapiro is freely given.

The manuscripts are not listed in the checklist. The largest and almost complete collection is in the Library of the University of Pennsylvania; the manuscript of *Sister Carrie* is in the New York Public Library; *Dawn* is in the Library of Indiana University. The Articles about Dreiser section includes chapters from, and material in, books.

H. C. A.

Contents

Contents

Major Works

America Is Worth Saving. New York: Modern Age, 1941.
292 pp. New York: The American Peace Movement
edition, (paper) 1941; Toronto: George T. McLeod, 1941.
Translations: *Spanish*, Buenos Aires: La Cruz del Sur,
1941.

An American Tragedy. 2 volumes, New York: Boni and
Liveright, 1925. Also issued in a limited, numbered and
signed edition in 1926. The first English edition, London:
Constable, 1926. A one volume edition, New York:
H. Liveright, 1929, reprinted Garden City, N. J.: Garden
City, 1934; reissued with a preface by H. L. Mencken,
Cleveland: World, 1946. Limited Editions Club published
an edition in 1954 with illustrations by Reginald Marsh.
An English Language edition was published in Moscow by
the Foreign Languages Publishing House in 1947. Other
editions include: New York: New American Library
(abridged), intro. George Mayberry, 1949; New York:
Modern Library (Giant), 1956; Cleveland: World, 1962,
intro. Robert Penn Warren; New York: Dell, 1962,
intro. Alfred Kazin; New York: New American Library,
1964, intro. Irving Howe. Translations: *Arabic*: al-
Qāhirah: al-Dar al-Qawmiyyah. lel-Tibā ah wa al-Nash,
1959. *Bohemian*: Prague: ROD, 1952. *Danish*: Copen-

1

hagen: Gyldendal, 1960. *German*: Berlin: P. Zsolnay, 1927; Vienna: Buchemenschaft, Donauländ, 1959. Gütersloh: Bertelsmann Lesering, 1962; Hamburg, Vienna: Zsolnay, 1962; Berlin: Aufbau, 1962; Weimar: Aufbau, 1964; Berlin, Weimar: Aufbau, 1965. *Hebrew*: Tel-Aviv: Mizrahi, 1960. *Hungarian*: Budapest: Europa, 1961; Budapest: Magyar Heliko Kiado, 1964; Budapest: Europa, 1966; Novi Sad, Yugoslavia: Forum, 1966. *Italian*: Milan: Baldini and Catoldi, n. d. *Japanese*: Tokyo: Shinchô-sha, 1958, 1960, 1961; Tokyo: Kadokawa Shoten, 1963, 1965. *Kazah*: Alma-Ata: Kazgoslitizdat, 1960, 1962. *Korean*: Seoul: Bagyeongsa, 1960. *Lettish*: Riga: Latg sizdat, 1958; Riga Liesma, 1965. *Lithuanian*: Vil'njus: Vaga, 1964. *Norwegian*: Oslo. Gyldendal, 1958. *Rumanian*: Bucharest: Editura Pentru Literatura, 1954, 1961, 1965. *Russian*: Moscow: Goslitzdat, 1959; Jaroslavl: Izvestia, 1960; Kišinev: Kartja Moldovenjaske, 1965.

The Aspirant. New York: Random House, (Random House Poetry Quartos) 1929.

"Background for *An American Tragedy*," *Esquire*, L (October, 1958), pp. 155-157. (Missing chapter from "Prelude.")

Best Short Stories. Cleveland: World, 1947. 349 pp. Intro. Howard Fast; Reissued 1956 with new introduction by James T. Farrell. Reissued: Greenwich, Connecticut, Fawcett, 1961. Contains, Khat, Free, St. Columba and the River, McEwen of the Shining Slave Makers, The Shadow, A Doer of the Word, Nigger Jeff, The Old Neighborhood, Phantom Gold, My Brother Paul, The Lost Phoebe, Convention, Marriage for One, The Prince Who Was a Thief.

A Book About Myself. New York: Boni and Liveright, 1923.
    502 pp. Reissued 1931 as *Newspaper Days*. English edition,
    London: Constable & Company, 1929. Translations:
    German: Berlin: P. Zsolnay, 1932.

The Bulwark. Garden City, New York: Doubleday, 1946.
    337 pp. Reissued: New York: Popular Library, 1960.
    English edition, London: Constable, 1947. Translations:
    Dutch: Amsterdam: A. de Lange, 1947. *German*: Zurich:
    Humanitas Verlag, 1947 as *Solon der Quaker*; Berlin:
    Aufbau, 1961. *Lithuanian*: Vil' njus: Vaga, 1965. *Swedish*:
    Stockholm: Norstedt, 1947.

Chains: *Lesser Novels and Stories*. New York: Boni and Live-
    right, 1927. 425 pp. A limited, numbered, and signed
    edition followed the above. Contains: Sanctuary, The
    Hand, Chains, St. Columba and the River, Convention,
    Khat, Typhoon, The Old Neighborhood, Phantom Gold,
    Marriage for One, Fulfillment, the Victor, The Shadow,
    The Mercy of God, and The Prince Who was a Thief.
    English edition, London: Constable & Company, 1928.

The Color of a Great City. New York, Boni and Liveright,
    1923. 287 pp. English edition, London: Constable
    and Company, 1930.

Dawn. New York: Liveright, 1931. 589 pp. "A History of
    Myself (I)."

Dreiser Looks at Russia. New York: Liveright, 1928, 264 pp.
    English edition, London: Constable and Company. 1928.
    Translations: *German*: Berlin: P. Zsolnay, 1929 as . . .
    Sowjet-Russland. *Yiddish*: Warsaw, 1931 as *Di Kunst un
    Literatur in Sovjet-Rusland*.

Dreiser's Russia, 1928. Melbourne: H. E. Langridge, 1928.
    40 pp.

Epitaph: A Poem. New York: Heron Press, 1929. 59 pp.
Illustrated by Robert Fawcett.

The Financier. New York: Harper and Brothers, 1912. 779 pp.
Reprinted New York: Boni and Liveright, 19 , and New
York: A. L. Burt, 1915. The first English edition, London:
Harper, 1912.

The Financier (revised edition). New York: Boni and Live-
right, 1927. 511 pp. This edition was rewritten from the
1912 edition and shortened by 277 pages. The English edi-
tion, London: Constable, 1927. Reissued, Cleveland:
World, 1946. Other United States editions include New
York: Dell, 1961, intro. Alfred Kazin; New York:
New American Library, 1967, afterword by Lazzer Ziff.
Translations: *Georgian*: Tbilisi: Sabcota Sakartvelo, 1966.
German: See *Titan*. *Lithuanian*: Vil'njus: Goslitizdat,
1958; Vil'njus: Vaga, 1966. *Russian*: Kiev: Goslitizdat
Ukrainy, 1959. *Slovenian*: Ljubljana: Državna Založba
Solvenije, 1966. *Spanish*: Buenos Aires: Editorial Futuro,
1943.

Fine Furniture. New York: Random House, 1930, 35 pp.
Random House Prose Quartos.

Free and Other Stories. New York: Boni and Liveright, 1918.
369 pp. Brought out New York: Modern Library, 1918,
intro. Sherwood Anderson. Contains: Free, McEwen
of the Shining Slave Makers, Nigger Jeff, The Lost Phoebe,
The Second Choice, Old Rogaum and His Theresa, The
Cruise of the "Idlewild," Married, and When the Old
Century Was New.

A Gallery of Women. New York: Liveright, 1929, 2 volumes.
English edition, London: Constable & Company, 1930.
Other United States editions include: Greenwich,

Connecticut: Fawcett, 1962, intro. William C. Lengel. Translations: *German*: as *Die Frau: funfzehn Lebensschicksale*. *Polish*: Warsaw: "Swiat," 1933; *Serbian*: Rijeka: Otokar Kersovani, 1963, 1965.

The Genius. New York: John Lane, 1915. 736 pp. English edition: London: John Lane, 1915; Toronto: S. B. Gundy, 1915. Suppressed in 1916 by the "New York Society for the Prevention of Vice." Later American editions include New York: Boni & Liveright, 1923, with a preface by Dreiser; Cleveland: World, 1954. Constable & Company brought out an edition: London: 1928. Translations: *Albanian*: Tirane: Naim Frasheri, 1965. *Armenian*: Erevah: Ajpatrat, 1960, 1961. *Azerbeidian*: Baku: Azernešv, 1958. *Chinese*: Taipei: Ming Hwa Book Co., 1964. *German*: Berlin: P. Zsolnay, 1929. *Hebrew*: Tel-Aviv: n.p. 195-. *Lettish*: Riga: Latgosizdat, 1962, 1963. *Lithuanian*: Vil'njus: Goslitizdat, 1963. *Spanish*: Buenos Aires: Editorial Futuro, 1944.

The Hand of the Potter. New York: Boni and Liveright, 1918. 209 pp.

Hey Rub-a-Dub-Dub. New York: Boni and Liveright, 1920. 312 pp. English edition: London: Constable, 1931. Contains: Hey Rub-a-dub-dub, Change, Some Aspects of Our National Character, The Dream, The American Financier, The Toil of the Laborer, Personality, A Counsel to Perfection, Neurotic America and the Sex Impulse, Scenery—Its Value, Ideals, Morals, and the Daily Newspaper, Equation Inevitable, Phantasmagoria, Ashtoreth, More Democracy or Less? An Inquiry, The Essential Tragedy of Life, Life, Art and America, and The Court of Progress.

A Hoosier Holiday. New York: John Lane, 1916. 513 pp.
English edition: London: Constable & Company, 1932.
Another issue, New York: Boni and Liveright, 1922,
using the original sheets.

Jennie Gerhardt. New York: Harper, 1911. 732 pp. Reprints:
New York: Boni and Liveright, 1923; New York: A. L.
Burt, 1924. English editions: London: Harper, 1911;
London: Constable, 1922. Other United States editions
include: Garden City, N. J.: Garden City, 1954; Cleveland:
World, 1946; New York: Dell, 1963, intro. Alfred
Kazin. Translations: *Finnish*: Helsinki: Otava, 1960.
German: Berlin: P. Zsolnay, 1928; Frankfurt a. M.:
Buchergilde Gutenberg, 1958; Hamburg: Rowohlt, 1960;
Berlin, Weimar: Aufbau, 1965. *Italian*: Milan: ELI, 1945.
Lithuanian: Vil'njus: Goslitizdat, 1962. *Polish*: Warsaw:
Czytelnk, 1956. *Russian*: Krashojarsk: Izvestia ,1958;
Minsk: Akad. Nauk BSSR, 1959; Tăskent: Goslitizdat
UzSSR, 1959; Moscow: Izvestia, 1960. *Slovenian*:
Ljblijana; Državna založba Slovenije, 1964. *Spanish*:
Buenos Aires: Club del Libro A. L. A., 1941.

Moods, Cadenced and Declaimed. New York: Boni and
Liveright, 1926. 328 pp. The limited, numbered, and
signed edition preceded the trade edition. The trade edition
contains the additional poems. English edition: London:
Constable and Company, 1929.

Moods Philosophic and Emotional, Cadenced and Declaimed.
New York: Simon and Schuster, 1935. 423 pp.

My City. New York: Liveright, 1929

Plays of the Natural and Supernatural. New York: John Lane,
1916. 228 pp. Another issue, New York: Dodd, Mead,
1922. Later editions: New York: Boni and Liveright, first

1926 edition adds two plays: Phantasmagoria, and The Count of Progress. The Boni and Liveright second 1926 edition added a third play, The Dream. The following are included in the first printings: The Girl in the Coffin, The Blue Sphere, Laughing Gas, In the Dark, The Spring Recital, The Light in the Window, and Old Ragpicker. English editions, London: John Lane, 1916; London: Constable, 1930.

Sister Carrie. New York: Doubleday, Page, 1900. 557 pp. Not suppressed as stated by Mencken and Dreiser. Another printing New York: B. W. Dodge and Company, 1907; a third printing New York: Grosset and Dunlap, 1908. Another printing New York: Harper and Brothers, 1918, with a Publishers' Note. New York: Boni and Liveright printed again 1917 and 1921. All of these printings were from the same plates. New edition, New York: Modern Library, 1942, preface by Dreiser. In 1939 the Limited Editions Club brought out an edition with illustrations by Reginald Marsh and an introduction by Burton Rascoe. In England *Sister Carrie* was published London: Heinemann, 1901, extensively revised. Reissued, London: W. H. Smith, 1910; London: Grant Richards, 1912. Complete English edition, London: Constable, 1927. A later English edition London: Oxford University Press, 1965, intro. Michael Millgate. Later United States editions include: New York: Pocket Books, 1949 (abridged), intro. Maxwell Geismar; New York: Rinehart, 1957, intro. Kenneth S. Lynn; Sagamore Press, 1957, intro. James T. Farrell; Boston: Houghton Mifflin, 1959, intro. Claude Simpson; New York: Dell, 1960, intro. Alfred Kazin; New York: New American Library, 1962, afterword Willard Thorpe; New York; Harper and Row, 1965.

In 1968 *Sister Carrie* was published in a facsimile reprint of the Heinemann 1901 edition by Johnson Reprint, New York, with an introduction by Jack Salzman. Translations: *Bulgarian*: Sofia: NSOF, 1958; *Czech*: Bratislava: Mlade' leta', 1965; Tatran, 1966; *Danish*: Copenhagen: Glydendel, 1962; *Estonian*: Tallin: Estogosizdat 1960; *Georgian*: Tbilisi: Sabčota Sakartvelo, 1964 as *Keri*; *German*: Berlin: P. Zsolnay, 1929; Dusseldorf: Dt. Bücherbund, 1959; Munich: Kindler, 1963; Berlin, Weimar: Aufbau, 1963 1965; *Italian*: Milan: N. Moneta, 194- as *Il Lammino di Una Donna*; Milan: Rizzoli, 1957 as *Nostra Sorella Carrie*; Turin: Einaudi, 1963 as *Nostra Sorella Carrie*; *Japanese*: Tokyo: Kenkyusha, 1959; *Korean*: Seoul: Dong'a 'chul' pan'sa, 1959; *Lithuanian*: Vilnjus: Goslitizdat, 1958, 1961; *Polish*: Poznan: Poznanski, 1959; Poznan: Wydawn, 1961; *Portuguese*: Rio de Janerio: Livaria do Globo, 1946; Saõ Paulo: Boa Leitura, 1964 as *Carolina*; *Rumanian*: Bucharest: Editura pentru literatura universala, 1962; *Russian*: Groznyj: Cečeno-Ingus, 1958; Moscow: Goslitizdat, 1960; *Serbian*: Zagreb: Zura, 1961, 1963, as *Carrie*; *Spanish*: Buenos Aires: Ediciones Modern, 1941; *Ukranian*: Kiev: DNIPRO, 1964.

The Stoic. Garden City, New York: Doubleday, 1947. 310 pp. Reissued Cleveland: World, 1952. Translations: *Czech*: Praha: SNKLU, 1964; *Estonian*: Tallin: Estonian State Publishing House, 1957; *Italian*: Rome: Editori Riunit, 1963; *Serbian*: Rijeka; Otokar Kersovani, 1956.

Theodore Dreiser. New York: Dell, 1962. 320 pp. A collection of short stories, sketches, poems, letters, etc., edited with an introduction by James T. Farrell.

Theodore Dreiser: His Autobiography. Greenwich, Connecticut: Fawcett, 1965. 2 volumes. Reissue of *Dawn* and *A Book About Myself*.

The Titan. New York: John Lane, 1914. 551 pp. English editions, London: John Lane, 1914; London: Constable, 1928. Also Toronto: Bell and Cockburn, 1914. Other United States editions include: Cleveland: World, 1946; New York: Dell, 1959, intro. Alfred Kazin. Translations: *Bulgarian*: Sofia: Modern Art Publishing House, 1949; *Czech*: Bratislava: Slov. Spis., 1966; *German*: Berlin: P. Zsolnay, 1928 as the third volume in a three volume work; the first two volumes being *The Financier*; *Latvian*: Riga: Latvijas valsto izdeynieciba, 1951; *Lithuanian*: Vilnjus: Goslitizdat, 1959; *Russian*: Kiev: Goslitizdat Ukrainy, 1959; *Serbian*: Belgrade: Education Publishing House, 1949; *Slovak*: Prague: Statni nakladetelstvi kuasne literatury a umeni, 1962; *Spanish*: Buenos Aires: Editorial Futuro, 1945; *Slovene*: Rijeka: Otokar Kersovani, 1956.

Tragic America. New York: Liveright, 1931. 430 pp. The first edition was suppressed. Edition put on sale contained minor changes for the most part, seemingly dictated by a fear of libel suits. English Edition, London: Constable & Company, 1932. Translations: *German*: Berlin: P. Zsolnay, 1932. *Russian*: Moscow: State Publishing House for Belles-Lettres, 1952.

A Traveler at Forty. New York: Century, 1913. 623 pp. Also New York: Boni and Liveright, 1926. Reprinted by Century in 1923. First English edition, London: Grant Richards, 1914.

Twelve Men. New York: Boni and Liveright, 1919. 360 pp. Other United States editions include: Greenwich, Connec-

ticut: Fawcett, 1962, intro. William C. Lengel. English
edition, London: Constable & Company, 1930. Also Leip-
sig: Tauchnitz, 1931. Contains: Peter, A Doer of the
Word, My Brother, The Country Doctor, Culhane, the
Solid Man, A True Patriarch, De Maupassant, Jr., The
Village Feudists, Vanity, Vanity, The Mighty Rourke,
A Mayor and His People, and W. L. S.

Introductions, Prefaces and Miscellaneous Works

A Princes of Arcady by Arthur Henry. New York: Doubleday, Page, 1900. Final chapter by Dreiser.

Life in a Garrison Town by Oswald Fritz Bilse. 10th ed. New York: John Lane, 1914. Introduction.

Caius Gracchus by Odin Gregory (pseud.). New York: Boni and Liveright, 1920. Introduction.

Ebony and Ivory by Llewelyn Powys. New York: Harcourt, Brace, 1923. Preface.

Lilith by George Sterling. New York: Macmillan, 1926. Introduction.

Poorhouse Sweeney by Ed Sweeney. New York: Boni and Liveright, 1927. Introduction.

Tono-Bungay by H. G. Wells. New York: Duffield, 1927. "Sandgate Edition." Introduction.

Songs of Paul Dresser by Paul Dresser. New York: Boni and Liveright, 1927. Introduction by Dreiser and "On the Banks of the Wabash, Far Away" partially by Dreiser.

The Road to Buenos Ayres by Albert Londres. London: Constable, 1928. Introduction.

The Crime of Dr. Garine by Boris Sokoloff. New York: Convici-Friede, 1928. Introduction.

The Argonaut Manuscript Limited Edition of Frank Norris's Works, Vol. VIII .Garden City, New York: Doubleday, Doran, 1928. Introduction. *McTeague.*

The Symbolic Drawings of Hubert Davis for An American Tragedy by Theodore Dreiser by Hubert Davis. New York: Liveright, 1930. Foreword.

Harlan Miners Speak. New York: Harcourt, Brace, 1932. Testimony by Dreiser.

Forced Labor in the United States by Walter Wilson. New York: International Publishers, 1933. Introduction.

Magnificent Hadrian by Sulamith Ish- Kishor. New York: Minton, Balch, 1935. Introduction.

Waiting for Nothing by Tom Kromer. London: Constable, 1935. Introduction.

The Way of All Flesh by Samuel Butler. 2 vols., New York: Limited Editions Club, 1936. Introduction.

Of Human Bondage by Somerset Maugham. New Haven: Limited Editions Club, 1938. Introduction.

The Living Thoughts of Thoreau, ed. Theodore Dreiser. New York: Toronto: Longmans, Green, 1939.

Published Letters

"The Dreiser—[Rufus M.] Jones Correspondence," edited by
Gerhard Friedrich. In *Bulletin of the Friends Historical
Association*, V, 50 (1957), 23-34.

Letters of Theodore Dreiser, edited by Robert H. Elias. Philadelphia: University of Pennsylvania, 1959.

Letters to Louise, edited with commentary by Louise Campbell.
Philadelphia: University of Pennsylvania, 1959.

Ryurikov, B. "Pis'mo Draizera," *Literaturnaya Gazeta*, XXVII
(July 5, 1967), 5.

White, William. "Dreiser on Hardy, Henley, and Whitman:
An Unpublished Letter," *English Language Notes*, VI
(December 1968), 122-124.

Biographies

Dreiser, Helen. *My Life with Dreiser*. Cleveland: World, 1951.

Dudley, Dorothy. *Forgotten Frontiers: Dreiser and the Land of the Free*. New York: Harrison Smith, 1932, reprinted as *Dreiser and the Land of the Free*. New York: Beechhurst Press, 1946. English edition: *Dreiser and the Land of the Free*.

Elias, Robert H. *Theodore Dreiser, Apostle of Nature*. Philadephia: University of Pennsylvania, 1949.

Rascoe, Burton. *Theodore Dreiser*. New York: R. M. McBride, 1925.

———.*We Were Interrupted*. Garden City: Doubleday, 1947.

Swanberg, W. A. *Dreiser*. New York: Scribner, 1965.

Bibliographies

Atkinson, Hugh C. *The Merrill Checklist of Theodore Dreiser.* Columbus, Ohio: Charles Merrill Co., 1969.

Elias, Robert H. "Theodore Dreiser," in Jackson R. Bryer, ed. *Fifteen Modern American Authors.* Durham, North Carolina: Duke University Press, 1969, pp. 101-138.

Gerber, Philip L. *Theodore Dreiser.* New York: Twayne, 1964. "Selected Bibliography," p. 201-211.

Kazin, Alfred, and Shapiro, Charles, eds. *The Stature of Theodore Dreiser.* Bloomington, Indiana: Indiana University Press, 1955. "A Selected Bibliography of Dreiser Biography and Criticism," pp. 271-303.

Libman, Valentina A.; trans. by Robert V. Allen; ed. by Clarence Gohdes. "Draizer, Teodor," in *Russian Studies of American Literature: A Bibliography.* Chapel Hill: University of North Carolina Press, 1969, pp. 65-76.

MacDonald, Edward D. *A Bibliography of the Writings of Theodore Dreiser.* Forward by Theodore Dreiser. Philadelphia: Centaur Book Shop, 1928.

Miller, Ralph N. *A Preliminary Checklist of Books and Articles on Theodore Dreiser.* Kalamazoo: Western Michigan College Library, 1947.

Orton, Vrest. *Dreiserana: A Book about his Books*. New York: Chocorua Bibliographies, 1929.

Salzman, Jack. "Theodore Dreiser (1871-1945)," *American Literary Realism 1870-1910*, II (Summer 1969), 132-138.

Spiller, Robert E. et al. "Theodore (Herman Albert) Dreiser, 1871–1945," pp. 474-477. In *Literary History of the United States*, vol. 3. New York: Macmillan, 1948.

Periodical Appearances

Dreiser's work as a newspaperman in St. Louis, Chicago and Pittsburgh, and his contributions to the Toledo *Blade* are not listed, nor are the unsigned columns he contributed to the journals he himself published or edited: *The Delineator*, *Ev'ry Month*, and *The Bohemian*.

"An Address to Caliban," *Esquire*, II (September 1934), 20-21.

"Amelia E. Barr and Her Home Life," *Demorest's*, XXXV (March 1899), 103-104.

"America and Her Communists," *Time and Tide*, XII (October 1931), 1247-1248.

"America and the Artist," *Nation*, CXX (April 15, 1925), 423-425.

"America—and War," *Labor Defender*, VIII (August 1932), 143-157.

"America—and War," *Labor Defender*, VIII (September 1932), 169, 175.

"The American Press and Political Prisoners," *Daily Worker*, May 9, 1931, p. 6.

"American Sculptors," *New York Times Illustrated Magazine*, September 25, 1898, pp. 6-7.

"American Tragedies," *New York Herald Tribune Books*, June 10, 1928, pp. 1-2.

"An American Tragedy," *National Epic*, I (June 1936), 9.

"The American Water-Color Society," *Metropolitan*, VII (1898), 489-493.

"American Women as Successful Playwrights," *Success*, II (June 17, 1899), 485-486.

"American Women Violonists," *Success*, II (September 30, 1899), 731-732.

"American Women Who Are Winning Fame As Pianists," *Success*, II (November 4, 1899), 815.

"American Women Who Play the Harp," *Success*, II (June 24, 1899), 501-502.

"Americans Are Still Interested in Ten Commandments—For the Other Fellow," *New York Call Magazine*, March 13, 1921, p. 7.

"America's Greatest Portrait Painters," *Success*, II (February 11, 1899), 183-184.

"Anatole France: A Post-Mortem Five Years Later," *Tambour* (Paris), No. 5, November 1929, pp. 25-26.

"And Continueth Not," *Ainslee's*, II (December 1898), 477.

"Another American Tragedy," *Forum*, LXXXI (March 1929), xlviii-li.

"Answer to French Labor," *Direction*, II (January–February 1939), 19.

"Anthony Hope Tells a Secret," *Success*, I (1898), 12-13.

"Appearance and Reality," *American Spectator*, I (January 1933), 4. Also in *American Spectator Yearbook* (1939).

"Apples," *Pearson's*, X (October 1900), 336-340.

"Are We in America Leading the Way to a Golden Age in the World," *New York American*, Section E, May 22, 1927 p. 3.

"The Art of MacMonnies and Morgan," *Metropolitan*, VII (1898), 143-151.

"The Art Work of Irving R. Wiles," *Metropolitan*, VII (1898), 357-361.

"Artists' Studios," *Demorest's*, XXXIV (1898), 196-198.

"As a Realist Sees It," *New Republic*, V (December 25, 1915), 202-204.

"Ashtoreth," *Reedy's Mirror*, XXVIII (July 10, 1919), 456-457.

"Atkinson on National Land Reform," *Success*, III (January 1900), 4.

"Barcelona in August," *Direction*, I (November–December 1938), 4-5.

"Barcelons's Modernity Shines Through Battle Damage," *Philadelphia Bulletin*, September 12, 1938, p. 9.

"Benjamin Eggleston, Painter," *Ainslee's*, I (1898), 41-47.

"Best Motion Picture Interview Ever Written," *Photoplay*, XXXIV (August 1928), 32-35, 124-131.

"Birth and Growth of a Popular Song," *Metropolitan*, VIII (November 1898), 497-502.

"Black Sheep Number One: Johnny," *Esquire*, XXII (October 1944), 39, 156-160.

"Black Sheep Number Two: Otie," *Esquire*, XXII (November 1944), 65.

"Black Sheep Number Three: Bill," *Esquire*, XXII (December 1944), 118, 296-297.

"Black Sheep Number Four: Ethelda," *Esquire*, XXIII (January 1945) 85, 127.

"Black Sheep Number Five: Clarence," *Esquire*, XXIII (February 1945), 49, 129-130.

"Black Sheep Number Six: Harrison Barr," *Esquire*, XXIII (March 1945), 49, 131.

"The Blue Sphere," *Smart Set*, XLIV (December 1914), 245-252.

"Bondage," *Ainslee's*, III (April 1899), 293.

"At Boulder Dam," *New York Times*, April 11, 1932, p. 14.

"Brandywine the Picturesque," *Demorest's*, XXXIV (1898), 274-275.

"Butcher Rogaum's Door," *Reedy's Mirror*, XI (December 21, 1901), 15-17.

"C. C. Curran," *Truth*, XVIII (September 1899), 227-231.

"The Camera Club of New York," *Ainslee's*, IV (October 1899), 324-335.

"Can a Criminal Come Back to Society? No." *Smoker's Companion*, I (May 1927), 19, 82.

"Capitalism Fails, says Dreiser," *New York Times*, July 5, 1932, p. 18.

"The Career of a Modern Portia," *Success*, II (February 18, 1899), 205-206.

"Carrier Pigeons in War Time," *Demorest's*, XXXIV (1898), 222-223.

"Cattails—November," *American Spectator*, I (January 1933), 2.

"Challenge to the Creative Man," *Common Sense*, II (November 1933), 6-8. *Artists' and Writers' Chap Book*, December 15, 1933, pp. 9-11, 45-46.

"Champ Clark, The Man and His District," *Ainslee's*, V (June, 1900), 425-434.

"Change," *New York Call Magazine*, January 26, 1918, p. 1.

"Chauncey M. Depew," *Hearst's International-Cosmopolitan*, LXXIX (July 1925), 86-87, 184-185.

"The Chicago Drainage Canal," *Ainslee's*, III (February 1899), 53-61.

"The Child and the School," *American Spectator*, I (April 1933), 2.

"Christ Church, Shrewsbury," *New York Times Illustrated Magazine*, August 27, 1899, pp. 11-12.

"Christmas in the Tenements," *Harper's Weekly*, XLVI (December 6, 1902), 52-53.

"Citizens of Moscow," *Vanity Fair*, XXXI (October 1928), 55-56, 102, 104.

" 'The Cliff Dwellers'—A Note on the Painting by George Bellows," *Vanity Fair*, XXV (December 1925), 55, 118.

"The Color of Today," *Harper's Weekly*, XLV (December 14, 1901), 1272-1273.

"Comments on Film Arts Guild," *West 8th Street Film Guild Cinema*, February 1, 1929, pp. 6, 9.

24

"Concerning Bruce Crane," *Truth*, XVIII (June 1899), 143-147.

"Convention," *American Mercury*, VI (December 1925), 398-408.

"A Conversation," *Direction*, I (January 1938), 2-4, 28.

"The Country Doctor," *Harper's Monthly*, CXXXVII (July 1918), 193-202.

"The Cradle of Tears," *New York Daily News*, Magazine Section, March 27, 1904, p. 4. *Tom Watson's Magazine*, I (May 1905), 349-350.

"A Cripple Whose Energy Gives Inspiration," *Success*, V (February 1902), 72-73.

"The Dawn is in the East," *International Literature*, No. 11, November 1939, pp. 109-111. *Common Sense*, VIII (December 1939), 6-7.

"Delaware's Blue Laws," *Ainslee's*, VII (February 1901), 53-57.

"The Days of Surfeit," *American Spectator*, I (November 1932), 2-3.

"Deeper Than Man-Made Laws," *Hearst's Magazine*, XXI (June 1912), 2395.

"Denies Move in Suit Against Kahn," *New York Times*, Oct. 6, 1931, p. 8.

"Descent of the Horse, Tracing the Horse's History 2,000,000 Years," *Everybody's*, II (June 1900), 543-547.

"A Doer of the Word," *Ainslee's*, IX (June 1902), 453-459.

"The Dream," *Seven Arts*, II (July 1917), 319-333.

"Dreiser Analyzes the Rebellion of Women," *New York American*, February 5, 1928, Section E, p. 3.

"Dreiser, at 65, Hails Roosevelt on Peace," *New York Times*, August 30, 1936, section II, p. 3.

"Dreiser Defends Norris on Power," *New York Times*, July 2, 1931, p. 16.

"Dreiser Denies He is Anti-Semitic," *New Masses*, XV (April 30, 1935), 10-11.

"Dreiser Discusses Sister Carrie," *Masses & Mainstream*, VIII (December 1955), p. 20-22.

"Dreiser Discusses Dewey Plan," *New York Telegram*, September 28, 1929, p. 4.

"Dreiser Fights Judgment," *New York Times*, March 1, 1938, p. 17.

"Dreiser Gives Vivid Picture of Conditions in Spain," *Philadelphia Bulletin*, September 10, 1938, p. 7.

"Dreiser Here Says Miners Will Rebel," *New York Times*, November 13, 1931, p. 18.

"Dreiser Home, Sees Soviet Aims Gaining," *New York Times*, February 22, 1928, p. 9.

"Dreiser Looks at Russia," *New York World*, March 19, 1928, p. 13; March 20, 1928, p. 15; March 21, 1928, p. 15; March 22, 1928, p. 15; March 23, 1928, p. 15; March 24, 1928, p. 17; March 25, 1928, p. 6; March 26, 1928, p. 15; March 27, 1928, p. 15; March 28, 1928, p. 17.

"Dreiser, Now 67, Is Critic of Critics," *New York Times*, August 27, 1938, p. 16.

"Dreiser on Matrimonial Hoboes," *New York American*, March 11, 1928, Section E, p. 4.

"Dreiser on Scottsboro," *Labor Defender*, VI (June 1931), 108.

"Dreiser on the Communists," *Masses & Mainstream*, VIII (December 1955), 23-25.

"Dreiser Recounts Loyalist Tension," *New York Times*, September 11, 1938, p. 30.

"Dreiser Says Judge Evades Mine Issue," *New York Times*, November 12, 1931, p. 13.

"Dreiser Says NRA Is Training Public," *New York Times*, August 28, 1933, p. 19.

"Dreiser Sees a Chance Lost," *New York Times*, March 2, 1933, p. 15.

"Dreiser See No Progress," *New York Globe*, February 22, 1921, p. 6.

"Dreiser Threatens Suit," *New York Times*, April 9, 1931, p. 28.

"Dreiser Visits Barcelona," *New York Times*, July 31, 1938, p. 25.

"Dreiser Warns Films on 'American Tragedy,' " *New York Times*, July 8, 1931, p. 20.

"Dreiser's Tribute to Mike Quinn," *Daily Worker*, September 1, 1947, p. 11.

"E. Percy Morgan and His Work," *Truth*, XVIII (February, 1899), 31-35.

"The Early Adventures of Sister Carrie," *Colophon*, Part 5, January, 1931, pp. 1-4.

"Editorial Conference," *American Spectator*, I (September 1933), 1.

"Editorial Note," *American Spectator*, II (February 1934), 1.

"Edmund Clarence Stedman at Home," *Munsey's*, XX (March 1899), 931-938.

"Electricity in the Household," *Demorest's*, XXXV (January 1899), 38-39.

"The Epic Sinclair," *Esquire*, II (December 1934), 32-33, 178 178B-179.

"Equity Between Nations," *Direction*, I (September–October 1938), 5-6, 11.

"The Factory, Witherbee, Sidney A.," *1910*, No. 5, 1910.

"Fame Found in Quiet Nooks," *Success*, I (September 1898), 5-6.

"Fine Furniture," *Household Magazine*, XXIX (December 1929), 29-32.

"The First Reader," *New York World*, May 9, 1930, p. 11.

"The First Voyage Over; Observations and Impressions of a Naively Sophisticated Traveler at Forty," *Century*, LXXXVI (August 1913), 586-595.

"Five Moods in a Minor Key,"*Esquire*, III (March 1935), 25.

"Five Poems," *New York Post, The Literary Review*, December 20, 1924, p. 8.

"Fools For Love," *New York American*, August 28, 1927, Section E, p. 4.

"Fools of Success," *New York American*, July 31, 1927, Section E, p. 4.

"The Foremost of American Sculptors," *New Voice*, XVI (June 17, 1899), 4-5, 13.

"Foreword," *Direction*, I (December 1937), 2.

"Four Cases of Clyde Griffiths," *New York Times*, March 8, 1936, Section 9, pp. 1-2.

"Four Poems," *Smart Set*, XLIX (May 1916), 277-278.

"Four Poems, I. 'The Little Flowers of Love and Wonder,' II. 'Proteus,' III. 'For a Moment the Wind Died,' IV. 'Take Hands,' " *American Mercury*, I (January 1924), 8-10.

"Free," *Saturday Evening Post*, CXC (March 16, 1918), 13-15, 81-89.

"From New York to Boston by Trolley," *Ainslee's*, IV (August 1899), 74-84.

"Fruit Growing in America," *Harper's Monthly*, CI (November 1900) 859-868.

"Fulfillment," *Holland's Magazine*, XLIII (February 1924), 7-9, 31.

"The Girl in the Coffin," *Smart Set*, XLI (October 1913), 167-240.

"Glory Be! McGlathery," *Pictorial Review*, XXVI (January 1925), 5-7, 51-52, 71.

"A Golden Sorrow," *Saturday Evening Post*, CLXXI (January 28, 1899), 496.

"Good and Evil," *North American Review*, CCXLVI (Autumn 1938), 67-86.

"Good Roads for Bad," *Pearson's*, IX (May 1900), 387-395.

"A Great American Caricaturist," *Ainslee's*, I (1898), 336-341.

"The Great American Novel," *American Spectator*, I (December 1932), 1-2.

"Great Problems in Organization, III. The Chicago Packing Industry," *Cosmopolitan*, XXV (1898), 615-626.

"Group Here Scores Anti-Soviet Drive," *New York Times*, March 16, 1930, p. 7.

"The Hand," *Munsey's*, LXVI (May 1919), 679-688.

"The Harlem River Speedway," *Ainslee's*, II (1898), 49-56.

"Humanitarianism in the Scottsboro Case," *Contempo*, I (1931), 1.

"I Am Grateful to Soviet Russia," *Soviet Russia Today*, VI (November 1937), 11. *International Literature*, No. 12, December 1937, pp. 107-108.

"I Find the Real American Tragedy," *Mystery Magazine*, XI (February 1935), 9-11, 88-90; (March 1935), 22-23, 77-79; (April 1935), 24-26, 90-92; (May 1935), 22-24, 83-86; (June 1935), 20-21, 68-73.

"I Go to Harlan," *Labor Defender*, VII (December 1931), 233.

"Ida Hauchawout," *Century*, CVI (July 1923), 335-348.

"If Force Transmutes," *Demorest's*, XXXV (August 1899), 243.

"An Important Philanthropy," *Demorest's*, XXXV (July 1899), 215-217.

"In Keeping," *Demorest's*, XXXV (January, 1899), 37.

"In the Dark," *Smart Set*, XLIV (January 1915), 419-425.

"Individualism and the Jungle," *New Masses*, VII (January 1932), 1-2. *Crawford's Weekly*, January 3, 1932, p. 6.

"Intellectual Unemployment," *New Freeman*, II (March 11, 1931), 616-617.

"Interdependence," *Free World*, X (September 1945), 69-70.

"The Irish Section Foreman Who Taught Me How to Live," *Hearst's International*, XLVI (August 1924), 20-21, 118-121.

"Is America's Restlessness a Symbol of Hidden Power," *New York American*, April 10, 1927, Section E, p. 3.

"Is College Worth While? No!" *Your Life*, III (March 1938), 8-12.

"It Pays to Treat Workers Generously," *Success*, II (September 16, 1899), 691-692.

"The Harp," *Cosmopolitan*, XXIV (1898), 637-644.

"The Haunts of Bayard Taylor," *Munsey's*, XVIII (1898), 594-601.

"The Haunts of Nathaniel Hawthorne," *Truth*, XVII (September 21, 1898), 7-9.

"The Haunts of Nathaniel Hawthorne," *Truth*, XVII (September 28, 1898), 11-13.

"Have We Free Will? A Debate, II. If Man Is Free So Is All Matter," *Forum* XCVIII (December 1937), 301-304.

"He Became Famous in a Day," *Success*, II (January 28, 1899), 143-144.

"Henry Mosler, a Painter for the People," *Demorest's*, XXXIV (1898), 67-69.

"Hey Rub-A-Dub-Dub," *Nation*, CIX (August 30, 1919), 278-281.

"A High Priestess of Art," *Success*, I (1898), 55.

"His Life Given Up to Music," *Success*, II (February 4, 1899), 167-168.

"Historic Tarrytown," *Ainslee's*, I (1898), 25-31.

"Hollywood: Its Morals and Manners," *Shadowland*, V (November 1921), 37, 61-63; (December 1921), 51, 61; (January 1922), 43, 67; (February 1922), 53, 66.

"Hollywood Now," *McCall's*, XLVIII (September 1921), 8, 18, 54.

"The Home of William Cullen Bryant," *Munsey's*, XXI (May 1899), 240-246.

"The Horseless Age," *Demorest's*, XXXV (May 1899), 153-155.

"How William Dean Howells Climbed Fame's Ladder," *Success*, I (April 1899), 5-6.

"Human Documents from Old Rome," *Ainslee's*, III (June 1899), 586-596.

"Japanese Home Life," *Demorest's*, XXXV (April 1899), 123-125.

"Jealousy," *Harper's Bazaar*, August 1924, pp. 84-85.

"John Burroughs in His Mountain Hut," *New Voice*, XVI (August 19, 1899), 7, 13.

"Just What Happened When the Waters of the Hudson Broke into the North River Tunnel," *New York Daily News*, January 23, 1904, Magazine Section, pp. 6-7.

"Karl Bitter, Sculptor," *Metropolitan*, IX (February 1899), 147-152.

"Keep Moving or Starve," *Today*, I (March 3, 1934), 6-7, 22-23.

"Kismet," *Esquire*, III (January 1934), 29, 175-176.

"Laughing Gas," *Smart Set*, XLV (February 1915), 85-94.

" 'Law' in Capitalists' Hands in Labor War, Says Dreiser," *Knoxville News-Sentinel*, November 9, 1931, p. 11.

"Lawrence F. Earl," *Truth*, XX (February 1901), 27-30.

"Is Leon Trotsky Guilty?" *Modern Monthly*, X (March 1937), 5.

"A Leader of Young Mankind, Frank W. Gunsaulus," *Success*, II (December 15, 1898), 23-24.

"Legalizing Games of Chance," *New York Times*, (May 4, 1937), 24.

"Lenin," *International Literature*, Nos. 4–5 (April–May 1940), 82.

"A Lesson from the Aquarium," *Tom Watson's Magazine*, III (January 1906), 306-308.

"Lessons I Learned from an Old Man," *Your Life*, II (January 1938), 6-10.

"Letter," *International Literature*, No. 1, January 1933, 126.

"Letter," *International Literature*, No. 4, October 1933, 123.

"A Letter About Stephen Crane," *Michigan Daily* (Ann Arbor), November 27, 1921, Magazine Section, p. 1.

"Letter to Editor," *New York Times*, May 4, 1937, p. 24.

"Letter to Editor," *St. Louis Star*, July 11, 1913, 2.

"A Letter to the Outlander," *Outlander*, I (Spring 1933), 50.

"Life, Art and America," *Seven Arts*, I (February 1917), 363-389.

"Life at Sixty-Seven," *Rotarian*, LV (August 1939), 8-10.

"Life is to Be Learned from Life," *New York Call Magazine*, July 27, 1919, p. 2.

"Life Stories of Successful Men—No. 10, Philip D. Amour," *Success*, I (October 1898), 3-4.

"Life Stories of Successful Men—No. 11, Chauncey M. Depew," *Success*, I (November 1898), 3-4.

"Life Stories of Successful Men—No. 12, Marshall Field," *Success*, II (December 8, 1898), 7-8.

"The Light in the Window," *International*, X (January, 1916), 6-8, 32.

"Like the Good Deed," *New Masses*, XXI (December 15, 1936), 9.

"Lilly Edwards: An Episode," *Smart Set*, XL (June 1913), 81-86.

"Literary Lions I Have Met," *Success*, II (February 25, 1899), 223-224.

"Little Clubmen of the Tenements," *Puritan*, VII (February 1900), 665-672.

"The Log of an Ocean Pilot," *Ainslee's*, III (July 1899), 683-692.

"The Loneliness of the City," *Tom Watson's Magazine*, II (October 1905), 474-475.

"The Lost Phoebe," *Century*, XCI (April 1916), 885-896.

"Love," *New York Tribune*, May 18, 1919, Part VII, 2-3. *Live Stories*, XXV (December 1920), 3-19.

"The Love Affairs of Little Italy," *New York Daily News*, April 10, 1904, Magazine Section, p. 3.

"The Making of Small Arms," *Ainslee's*, I (1898), 540-549.

"The Making of Stained-Glass Windows," *Cosmopolitan*, XXVI (January 1899), 243-252.

"A Man and His House," *Hoggson Magazine*, III (June 1917), 107.

"Man and Romance," *Reedy's Mirror*, XXVIII (August 28, 1919), 585. *New York Call Magazine*, September 14, 1919, p. 9.

"Mark the Double Twain," *English Journal*, XXIV (October 1935), 615-627.

"Mark Twain: Three Contacts," *Esquire*, IV (October 1935), 22, 162, 162A, 162B.

"Marriage and Divorce," *Forum*, LXIV (July 1920), 26-36.

"Married," *Cosmopolitan*, LXIII (September 1917), 31-35, 112-115.

"The Martyr," *American Spectator*, I (July 1933), 4.

"A Master of Photography," *Success*, II (June 10, 1899), 471.

"Mathewson," *Esquire*, I (May 1934), 20-21, 125; (June 1934), 24-25, 114.

"A Mayor and His People," *Era*, XI (June 1903), 578-584.

"The Meaning of the USSR in the World Today," *Soviet Russia Today*, IX (November 1940), 23, 47. *Current History*, LII (December 10, 1940), 28-30.

"The Meddlesome Decade," *Theatre Guild Magazine*, VI (May 1929), 11-13, 61-62.

"The Men in the Dark," *American*, LXXIII (February 1912), 465-468.

"The Mercy of God," *American Mercury*, II (August 1924), 457-464.

"Message to Congress," *Direction*, II (May–June 1939), 2.

"The Mighty Burke," *McClure's*, XXXVII (May 1911), 40-50.

"Mr. Dreiser and the Broadway Magazine," *The Review*, II (June 5, 1920), 597.

"Mr. Dreiser Denies Report," *New York Times*, August 15, 1934, p. 16.

"Mr. Dreiser Excepts," *New York Times*, March 15, 1928, p. 24.

"Mr. Dreiser Replies," *New York Herald-Tribune Books*, February 14, 1932, p. 18.

"A Monarch of Metal Workers," *Success*, II (June 3, 1899), 453-454.

"Mooney and America," *Hesperian*, I (Winter 1930), 2-4.

"More Cargoes," *Saturday Evening Post*, CLXXI (December 10, 1898), 384.

"More Democracy or Less: An Inquiry," *New York Call Magazine*, November 30, 1919, pp. 6-7. *Reconstruction*, I (December 1919), 338.

"Mortuarium," *Demorest's*, XXXIV (1898), 279.

"The Most Successful Ball-Player of Them All," *Hearst's International*, XLVII (February 1925), 82-83, 102-106.

"The Muffled Oar," *Nation*, CXXVIII (February 27, 1929), 258.

"Music," *Vanity Fair*, XXVI (June 1926), 68.

"My City," *New York Herald Tribune*, December 23, 1928, Section III, p. 1.

"My Favorite Fiction Character," *Bookman*, LXIII (April 1926), 175.

"Myself and the Movies," *Esquire*, XX (July 1943), 50, 159.

"The Myth of Individuality," *American Mercury*, XXXI (March 1934), 337-342.

"Neither Devil nor Angel," *New Republic*, III (July 10, 1915), 262-263.

"The New Humanism," *Thinker*, II (July 1930), 8-10.

"The New Knowledge of Weeds," *Ainslee's*, VIII (January 1902), 533-538.

"New York's Underground Railroad," *Pearson's*, IX (April 1900), 375-384.

"Nigger Jeff," *Ainslee's*, VIII (November 1901), 366-375.

"Night Son," *Ainslee's*, II (1898), 73.

"No Sitting in the Shade for Dreiser at 63," *New York Times*, August 28, 1934, p. 19.

"The Old Neighborhood," *Metropolitan*, XLIX (December 1918), 27-30, 46, 48-50.

"The Old 10:30 Train," *Tom Watson's Magazine*, I (March 1905), 96.

"Olive Brand," *Hearst's International-Cosmopolitan*, LXXXIV (May 1928), 47-49, 130-134.

"On the Field at Brandywine," *Truth*, XVI (November 6, 1897), 7-10.

"On the Soviet-Finnish Peace Treaty," *Soviet Russia Today*, VIII (April 1940), 8.

"Our Amazingly Illusioned Press," *New York Call Magazine*, December 16, 1917, p. 3.

"Our Democracy: Will It Endure?" *New Masses*, XXXVIII (January 21, 1941) 8-9.

"Our Greatest Writer Tells What's Wrong With Our Newspapers," *Pep*, II (July 1917), 8-9.

"Our Women Violinists," *Puritan*, II (November 1897), 34-35.

"Out of My Newspaper Days, I. 'Chicago,' " *Bookman*, LIV (November 1921), 208-217.

"Out of My Newspaper Days, II. 'St. Louis,' " *Bookman*, LIV (January 1922), 427-433.

"Out of My Newspaper Days, III. ' "Red" Galvin,' " *Bookman*, LIV (February 1922), 542-550.

"Out of My Newspaper Days, IV. 'The Bandit,' " *Bookman*, LV (March 1922), 12-19.

"Out of My Newspaper Days, V. 'I Quit the Game,' " *Bookman*, LV (April 1922), 118-125.

"A Notable Colony: Artistic and Literary People of the Picturesque Bronx," *Demorest's*, XXXV (August 1899), 240-241.

"Overland Journey," *Esquire*, IV (September 1935), 24, 97.

"A Painter of Cats and Dogs," *Demorest's*, XXXV (February 1899), 68-69.

"A Painter of Travel," *Ainslee's*, I (1898), 391-398.

"Paris," *Century*, LXXXVI (October 1913), 904-915.

"Paris—1926," *Vanity Fair*, XXVII (December 1926), 64, 136, 147-150.

"Phantom Gold," *Live Stories*, XXVI (February 1921), 3-23.

"A Photographic Talk with Edison," *Success*, I (February 1898), 8-9.

"Plant Life Underground," *Pearson's*, XI (June 1901), 860-864.

"Portrait of a Woman," *Bookman*, LXVI (September 1927), 2-14.

"Portrait of an Artist," *Vanity Fair*, XXXII (April 1929), 70, 108, 110.

"The Problem of the Soil," *Era*, XII (September 1903), 239-249.

"The Profit Makers Are Thieves," *Common Sense*, II (December 1933), 20-22.

"A Prophet, But Not Without Honor," *Ainslee's*, I (1898), 73-79.

"Prosperity for Only One Percent of the People," *Daily Worker*, January 28, 1931, p. 1.

"The Pushcart Man," *New York Call Magazine*, March 30, 1919, p. 1, 7.

"The Question of Literary Censorship," *Independent*, CX (March 17, 1923), 191.

"The Railroad and the People. A New Educational Policy Now Operating in the West," *Harper's Monthly*, C (February 1900), 479-484.

"Rally Round the Flag," *Common Sense*, III (May 1934), 23.

"The Real Choate," *Ainslee's*, III (April 1899), 324-333.

"The Real Howells," *Ainslee's*, V (March 1900), 137-142.
   Americana, XXXVII (April 1943), 274-283.

"The Real Sins of Hollywood," *Liberty*, IX (June 11, 1932),
   6-11.

"Recent Poems of Life and Labour," *Vanity Fair*, XXVI
   (August 1926), 61.

"Recent Poems of Love and Sorrow," *Vanity Fair*, XXVII
   (September 1926), 54.

"Recent Poems of Youth and Age," *Vanity Fair*, XXVII
   (October 1926), 70.

"Regina C—," *Hearst's International-Cosmopolitan*, LXXXIV
   (June 1928), 56-58, 144-149.

"Reina," *Century*, CVI (September 1923), 695-716.

"Rella," *Hearst's International-Cosmopolitan*, LXXXIV (April
   1928), 36-39, 199-204.

"A Remarkable Art," *Great Round World*, XIX (May 3, 1902),
   430-434.

"Remarks," *Psychoanalytic Review*, XVIII (July 1931), 250.

"The Return," *Ainslee's*, II (1898), 280.

"The Right to Kill," *New York Call Magazine*, March 16, 1918,
   pp. 1, 12-13.

"The Rights of a Columnist," *Nation*, CXXVI (May 30, 1928),
   608.

"The Rivers of the Nameless Dead," *Tom Watson's Magazine*,
   I (March 1905), 112-113.

"Road to Life," *Worker* (April 16, 1950), Section 1, p. 9.

"The Romance of Power," *Vanity Fair*, **XXIX** (September 1927), 49, 94, 96, 98.

"Rural America in War-Time," *Scribner's*, **LXIV** (December 1918), 734-746.

"Rural Free Mail Delivery," *Pearson's*, **XI** (February 1901), 233-240.

"Russia, The Great Experiment," *Vanity Fair*, **XXX** (June 1928), 47-48, 102.

"The Russian Advance," *Soviet Russia Today*, **XIII** (July 1944), 9.

"Russian Vignettes," *Saturday Evening Post*, **CC** (April 28, 1928), 18-19, 80-82.

"The Saddest Story," *New Republic*, **III** (June 12, 1915), 155-156.

"Sanctuary," *Smart Set*, **LX** (October 1919), 35-52.

"Says Roosevelt Uses Karl Marx's Ideas," *New York Times*, August 22, 1938, p. 3.

"Scared Back to Nature," *Harper's Weekly*, **XLVII** (May 16, 1903), 816.

"Scenes in a Cartridge Factory," *Cosmopolitan*, **XXV** (1898), 321-324.

"The Scope of Fiction," *New Republic*, **XXX** (April 12, 1922), Part II, 8-9.

"The Sculpture of Fernando Mirando," *Ainslee's*, **II** (August 1898), 113-118.

"The Second Choice," *Cosmopolitan*, LXIV (February 1918), 53-58, 104, 106-107.

"The Seventh Commandment," *Liberty*, IX (April 9, 1932), 34-38.

"Sherwood Anderson," *Clipper*, II (May, 1941), 5. *Story*, XIX (September–October 1941), 4.

"The Shining Slave Makers," *Ainslee's*, VII (June 1901), 445-450.

"Six O'Clock," *1910*, No. 4, 1910.

"The Smallest and Busiest River in the World," *Metropolitan*, VII (1898), 355-363.

"Solution," *Woman's Home Companion*, LX (November 1933), 19-20, 132-135.

"Sombre Annals," *New York Post, The Literary Review*, November 17, 1923, p. 255.

"Soviet Plan to Spread to U. S. Dreiser Thinks," *New York World*, March 18, 1928, pp. 1, 8.

"The Soviet-Finnish Treaty and World Peace," *Soviet Russia Today*, VIII (April 1940), 8-9.

"The Sowing," *Ainslee's*, XIII (April 1904), 135.

"The Spring Recital," *Little Review*, II (December 1915), 28-35.

"The Standard Oil Works at Bayonne," *New York Call Magazine*, March 16, 1919, pp. 3, 5.

"A Start in Life," *Scribner's*, XCVI (October 1934), 211-217.

"Statement of Belief," *Bookman*, LXVIII (September 1928), 25.

"The Story of a Human Nine-Pin," *New York Daily News*, April 3, 1904, Magazine Section, p. 3.

"The Story of a Song-Queen's Triumph," *Success*, III (January 1900), 6-8.

"The Story of Harry Bridges," *Friday*, I (October 4, 1940), 1-8, 28; (October 11, 1940), 14-17.

"The Story of the States: No. III—Illinois," *Pearson's*, XI (April 1901), 513-543.

"Studies of Public Characters II—The Real Zangwill," *Ainslee's*, II (November 1898), 351-357.

"Supplication," *Demorest's*, XXXIV (1898), 302.

"A Symposium of American Writers and Scholars on Goethe," *Monatshefte fur Deutschen Unterricht*, XXIV (March–April 1932), pp. 75-93.

"Symposium on the Medical Profession," *Medical Review of Reviews*, XXIII (January 1917), 8-9.

"Tabloid Tragedy," *Hearst's International-Cosmopolitan*, XCV (December 1933), 22-25, 115-116, 119-121.

"Take a Look at our Railroads," *Liberty*, VIII (November 7, 1931), 24-27.

"A Talk With America's Leading Lawyer," *Success*, I (January 1898), 40-41.

"Temperaments—Artistic and Otherwise," *Golden Book*, XIX (June 1934), 650-654.

"Tempted, I Stole," *Hearst's International-Cosmopolitan*, XC (June 1931), 48-49, 196.

"The Tenement Toilers," *Success*, V (April 1902), 213-214, 232. *New York Call Magazine*, August 24, 1919, pp. 6-7.

"Theodore Dreiser and the Free Press," *People's World*,
October 2, 1940, p. 5.

"Theodore Dreiser Condemns War," *People's World*, April 6,
1940, p. 7.

"Theodore Dreiser Defends His Brother's Memory," *New
York Post*, March 27, 1936, p. 14.

"Theodore Dreiser Finds Both Hope and Failure in Russian
Soviet Drama," *Chicago Daily News*, February 1928,
pp. 1-2.

"Theodore Dreiser on the Elections," *New Masses*, IV
(November 1928), 17.

"Theodore Dreiser Picks the Six Worst Pictures of the Year,"
New Movie Magazine, V (January 1932), 25-27, 98.

"Theodore Dreiser Snubs Hoover," *People's World*, January
12, 1940, pp. 1, 6.

"These United States, XXXIX, 'Indiana, Her Soil and Light,'"
Nation, CXVII (October 3, 1923), 348-350. *These
United States: A Symposium, Second Series*, ed. Ernest
Gruening, 1924.

"This Florida Scene," *Vanity Fair*, XXVI (May 1926), 61, 100,
110; (June 1926), 43, 98, 100; (July 1926), 63, 94, 96.

"This is Churchill's 'Democracy,'" *New Masses*, XXXVIII
(February 18, 1941), 35-36.

"This Madness—An Honest Novel About Love," *Hearst's
International-Cosmopolitan*, LXXXVI (February 1929),
22-27, 192-203; (March 1929), 44-47, 160-166; (April
1929), 81-85, 117-120; (May 1929), 80-83, 146-154;
(June 1929), 83-87, 156-168; (July 1929), 86-87, 179-186.

"Thomas Brackett Reed: The Story of a Great Career," *Success*, III (June 1900), 215-216.

"Thou Giant," *Success*, I (September 1898), 16.

"Three Poems, 'Evening—Mountains,' 'Chief Strong-Bow Speaks,' 'Love,' " *American Spectator*, II (February 1934), 4.

"Three Sketches of the Poor," *New York Call*, November 23, 1913, p. 10.

"Through All Adversity," *Demorest's*, XXXIV (1898), 334.

"The Tithe of the Lord," *Esquire*, X (July 1938), 36-37, 150, 155-158.

"To Him I Owe Very Much," *Political Affairs*, XXX (March 1951), 95-96.

"To Make It Safe For Art," *Reedy's Mirror*, XXVIII (February 21, 1919), 101-102.

"The Toil of the Laborer," *New York Call*, July 13, 1913, p. 11. *Reconstruction*, I (October 1919), 310-313.

"A Touch of Human Brotherhood," *Success*, V (March 1902), 140-141, 176.

"The Town of Pullman," *Ainslee's*, III (March 1899), 189-200.

"Townsend," *American Spectator*, I (June 1933), 2.

"The Trade of the Mississippi," *Ainslee's*, IV (January 1900), 735-743.

"The Transmigration of the Sweat Shop," *Puritan*, VIII (July 1900), 498-502.

"The Treasure House of Natural History," *Metropolitan*, VIII (1898), 595-601.

"Tribute to Gorky," *Soviet Russia Today*, V (July 1936), 7.

"True Art Speaks Plainly," *Booklover's Magazine*, I (February 1903), 129. *Modernist*, I (November 1919), 21.

"An Uncommercial Traveler in London," *Century*, LXXXVI (September 1913), 736-749.

"U. S. Must Not be Bled for Imperial Britain," *People's World*, November 12, 1940, p. 6 .

Untitled, *The Magazine of Sigma Chi*, LXIII (October–November 1944), 39-40.

"Upton Sinclair," *Clipper*, I (September 1940), 3-4.

"V. I. Lenin," *New Masses*, XXXV (April 23, 1940), 16.

"The Victim Speaks," *Vanity Fair*, XXVII (February 1927), 40.

"Virtue," *Demorest's*, XXXIV (1898), 100.

"A Vision of Fairy Lamps," *Success*, I (March 1898), 23.

"The Voyage," *Ainslee's*, XIV (October 1904), 136.

"The Wages of Sin," *Hearst's International-Cosmopolitan*, LXXXI (October 1926), 42-45, 175-181.

"What Has the Great War Taught Me?" *New Masses*, XII (August 7, 1934), 15.

"What I Believe; 'Living Philosophies—III,' " *Forum*, LXXXII (November 1929), 279-281, 317-320.

"What Is Americanism?" *Partisan Review and Anvil*, III (April 1936), 3-4.

"What Is Democracy?" *Clipper*, I (December 1940), 3-7.

"What To Do, With Apologies to Leo Tolstoy," *Free World*, IX (March 1945), 10.

"When the Old Century Was New; a Love Story," *Pearson's*, XI (January 1901), 131-140.

"When the Sails Are Furled: Salior's Snug Harbor," *Ainslee's*, II (1898), 593-601. *New York Tribune Sunday Magazine*, May 22, 1904, pp. 3-5, 19.

"Whence the Song," *Harper's Weekly*, XLIV (December 8, 1900), 1165-1169.

"Where Battleships are Built," *Ainslee's*, I (1898), 433-439.

"Where is Labor's Share?" *New York Times*, May 13, 1931, p. 24.

"Where We Stand," *International Literature*, No. 3, July 1934, p. 80.

"Who Challenges the Social Order? Applied Religion—Applied Art," *Survey*, L (May 1, 1923), 175.

"Who Wills To Do Good," *Ainslee's*, II (January 1899), 667.

"Whom God Hath Joined Together," *Plain Talk*, VI (April 1930), 401-404.

"Why I Joined the Communist Party," *Worker*, December 28, 1947, Magazine Section, p. 11.

"Why Not Tell Europe About Bertha Clay," *New York Call*, October 24, 1921, p. 6.

"Why the Indian Paints His Face," *Pearson's*, XI (January 1901), 19-23.

"Will Fascism Come to America?" *Modern Monthly*, VIII (September 1934), 459-461.

"Winterton," *American Spectator*, II (December 1933), 3-4.

"Women Are the Realists," *You*, II (Fall 1939), 5, 48-49.

"Women Who Have Won Distinction in Music," *Success*, II (April 8, 1899), 325-326.

"Woodmen," *Demorest's*, XXXV (May 1899), 159.

"Woods Hole and the Marine Boilogical Laboratory," *Collecting Net*, III (July 21, 1928), 1-2.

"A Word Concerning Birth Control," *Birth Control Review*, V (April 1921), 5-6, 12-13.

"Work of Mrs. Kenyon Cox," *Cosmopolitan*, XXIV (1898), 477-480.

"A Writer Looks at the Railroads," *American Spectator*, I March 1933), 4.

"You, the Phantom," *Esquire*, II (November 1934), 25-26.

Books and Dissertations About Dreiser

Antush, John V. *Money in the Novels of James Wharton, and Dreiser*. Ph.D. Dissertation, Stanford University, 1968.

Arnavon, Cyrille. *Théodore Dreiser: Romancier American*. Paris: Université de Lille, Centre de Documentation Universitaire, 1956.

Biddle, Edmund R. *The Plays of Theodore Dreiser*. Ph.D. Dissertation, University of Pennsylvania, 1965.

Bizam, Lenke. *Theodore Dreiser*. Budapest: Gondolat, 1963.

Blacksin, Ida. *Theodore Dreiser and the Law*. M.A. Thesis, New York University, 1948.

Bower, Marie Hadley. *Theodore Dreiser: The Man and His Times: His Work and Its Reception*. Ph.D. Dissertation, The Ohio State University, 1940.

Broderick, John C. *Theodore Dreiser's "Sister Carrie."* Bound Brook, N. J.: Shelley Pub. Co., 1963.

Davis, Joe. *The Mind of Theodore Dreiser: A Study in Development*. Ph.D. Dissertation, Emory University, 1961.

Dowell, Richard W. *Theodore Dreiser and Success*: *A Shifting Allegiance*. Ph.D. Dissertation, Indiana University, 1968.

Dustman, Marjory P. *Theodore Dreiser's "An American Tragedy"*: *A Study*. Ph.D. Dissertation, University of Southern California, 1965.

Elias, Robert H. *Theodore Dreiser: Apostle of Nature*. Philadelphia: University of Pennsylvania Press, 1949.

Elveback, Helen B. *The Novels of Theodore Dreiser with an Analysis of His Other Writings*. Ph.D. Dissertation, University of Minnesota, 1946.

Gerber, Philip L. *Theodore Dreiser*. New York: Twayne, 1964. Twayne's United States Author series, 52.

Greenberg, Emil. *A Case Study in the Technique of Realism*: *Theodore Dreiser's "An American Tragedy."* M.A. Thesis, New York University, 1936.

Hakutani, Yoshinobu. *Dreiser Before "Sister Carrie": French Realism and Early Experience*. Ph.D. Dissertation, Pennsylvania State University, 1965.

Howell, Eileen. *Theodore Dreiser's Development as a Naturalist*. M.A. Thesis, New York University, 1950.

Hussman, Lawrence E. *The Spiritual Quest of Theodore Dreiser*. Ph.D. Dissertation, University of Michigan, 1964.

Jones, Alan K. *The Family in the Works of Theodore Dreiser*. Ph.D. Dissertation, Texas Technical College, 1969.

Kazin, Alfred and Charles Shapiro, eds. *The Stature of Theodore Dreiser*. Bloomington: Indiana University Press, 1955, 1965.

Lehan, Richard. *Theodore Dreiser*: *His World and His Novels*. Carbondale: Southern Illinois University Press, 1969.

Levine, Richard. *Characterization in Dreiser's Fiction*. M.A. Thesis, New York University, 1951.

Lundkvist, Artur. *Tre Amerikaner: Dreiser—Lewis—Anderson*. Stockholm: A. Bonnier, 1939.

McAleer, John J. *Theodore Dreiser; An Introduction and Interpretation*. New York: Holt, 1968.

McCall, Raymond G. *Attitudes Towards Wealth in the Fiction of Theodore Dreiser, Edith Wharton and F. Scott Fitzgerald*. Ph.D. Dissertation, University of Wisconsin, 1957.

Maillard, Denyse. *L'Enfant American dans le Roman du Middle-West*. Ph.D. Dissertation, Universitie de Paris, 1935.

Matthiessen, F. O. *Theodore Dreiser*. New York: Sloane, 1951.

Miller, Raymond A. Jr. *Representative Tragic Heroines in the Work of Brown, Hawthorn, Howells, James, and Dreiser*. Ph.D. Dissertation, University of Wisconsin, 1957.

Moers, Ellen. *Two Dreisers*. New York: Viking, 1969.

Nedic, Borivoje. *Tedor Drajzer*. Moscow: 1964.

Nostwich, Theodore D. *The Structure of Theodore Dreiser's Novels*. Ph.D. Dissertation, University of Texas, 1969.

Rothweiler, Robert Liedel. *Ideology and Four Radical Novelists: The Response to Communism of Dreiser, Anderson, Dos Passos, and Farrel*. Ph.D. Dissertation, Washington University, 1960.

Salzman, Jack. *"Sister Carrie": A History of Dreiser's Novel*. Ph.D. Dissertation, New York University, 1966.

Samuels, Charles. *Death Was the Bridegroom*. New York: 1955.

Schmidberger, Loren Francis. *The Structure of the Novels of Theodore Dreiser.* Ph.D. Dissertation, Fordham University, 1965.

Schmidt-von Bardeleben, Renate. *Das Bild New Yorks in Erzählwerk von Dreiser und Dos Passos.* (Mainzer Amerikanistische Beitrage 9) München: HueberVerl., 1967.

Shapiro, Charles K. *A Critical Study of the Novels of Theodore Dreiser,* Ph.D. Dissertation, Indiana University, 1959.

―――. *Guide to Theodore Dreiser.* Columbus, Ohio: Charles E. Merrill, 1969.

―――. *Theodore Dreiser: Our Bitter Patriot.* Carbondale: Southern Illinois University Press, 1962.

Springer, Anne Marie. *The American Novel in Germany: A Study of the Critical Reception of Eight American Novelists Between the Two World Wars.* Ph.D. Dissertation, University of Pennsylvania, 1959.

Staab, Wolfgang. *Das Deutschlandbild Theodore Dreisers.* Mainz: 1961.

Stepanchev, Stephen. *Dreiser Among the Critics.* Ph.D. Dissertation, New York University, 1950.

Takagaki, Matsuo. *Theodore Dreiser.* Tokyo: 1933.

Takamura, Katsuji, ed. *Dreiser.* Tokyo: Kenkyusha, 1967.

Tjader, Marguerite. *Theodore Dreiser, A New Dimension.* Norwalk, Conn.: Silvermine, 1965.

Wilkinson, Robert E. *A Study of Theodore Dreiser's "The Financier."* Ph.D. Dissertation, University of Pennsylvania, 1965.

Willen, Gerald. *Dreiser's Moral Seriousness: A Study of the Novels*. Ph.D. Dissertation, University of Minnesota, 1956.

Winzberger, Karl-Heinz. *Die Romaine Theodore Dreisers*. Berlin: Deutscher verlag der Wissenchafter, 1955.

Zasurskij, Ja. *Teodor Drajzer*, Moscow: University Press, 1964.

———. *Teodor Drajzer: Pisatel Publitsist*. Moscow: 1957.

——— and Roman Samarin. *Teodor Drajzer v Bor'be Protiv Amerikanskogo Imperializma*. Moscow: 1952.

Articles About Dreiser

Attention is directed to *The Dreiser Newsletter* (volume I, 1970), edited by Richard W. Dowell and Robert P. Saalbach, English Department, Indiana State University, Terre Haute, Indiana.

Aaron, Daniel. *Writers on the Left.* New York: Harcourt, Brace & World, 1961, pp. 8 ff.

Adams, James Donald. "The Heavy Hand of Dreiser," *The Shape of Books to Come.* New York: Viking, 1944, pp. 54-83.

————. The *Writer's Responsibility.* London: Secker and Warburg, 1946, pp. 54 ff.

Adcock, A. St. John. "Theodore Dreiser," *The Glory That Was Grub Street.* London: Silow Marston, 1928, pp. 43-52.

Adler, Elmer, ed. *Breaking Into Print.* New York: Simon and Schuster, 1937, pp. 66-67.

Åhnebrink, Lars. *The Beginnings of Naturalism in American Fiction.* Uppsala: Lundequistska Bokhandeln, 1950, pp. 7 ff.

————. "Garland and Dreiser: An Abortive Friendship," *Midwest Journal*, VII (Winter 1955/6), 285-292.

———. "Dreiser's *Sister Carrie* and Balzac," *Symposium*, VII (November 1953), 306-322.

Allen, Walter, *The Modern Novel*. New York: Dutton, 1964, pp. 81-86.

Anderson, Sherwood. "An Apology for Crudity," *The Dial*, LXIII (November 8, 1917), 437-438.

———. "Dreiser," *Little Review*, III (April 1916), 54.

———. "Introduction," *Free and Other Stories*. New York: The Modern Library, 1925, pp. v-x.

———. *Sherwood Anderson's Memoirs*. New York Harcourt, Brace, 1942, pp. 165 ff.

———. *The Portable Sherwood Anderson*, ed. Horace Gregory. New York: Viking, 1949, pp. 557-559.

Anon. "American Writers Look Left," *London Times Literary Supplement*, February 22, 1936, pp. 145-46.

Anon. "Dark Blue Dreiser," *Literary Digest*, CVI (July 26, 1930), 17.

Anon. "Dreiser on the Sins of Hollywood," *Literary Digest*, CIX (May 2, 1931), 21.

Anon. "Dreiser the Great," *Newsweek*, XXVII (March 25, 1946), 102.

Anon. "Dreiser's Arraignment of Our Intellectual Aridity," *Current Opinion*, LXII (May 1917), 344-345.

Anon. "Dreiser's Feud with Kentucky," *Literary Digest*, CXI (November 28, 1931), 9.

Anon. "Dreiser's Novels as a Revelation of the American Soul," *Current Opinion*, LXII (May 1917), 191.

Anon. "Freer Verse Than Usual," *New York Times*, September 10, 1926, p. 4.

Anon. "Enemies of Society," *New Republic* LXIII (May 8, 1929), 318-320.

Anon. "The Liberation of American Literature," *London Times Literary Supplement*, June 15, 1933, pp. 401-402.

Anon. "Literary Lunch," *Literary Review*, IV (August 2, 1924), 936-937.

Anon. "Poor Dreiser," Bookman, LXXV (November 1932), 682-684.

Anon. "A Re-examination of Dreiser," *London Times Literary Supplement*, December 21, 1951, pp. 813-14.

Anon. "The Secret of Personality as Mr. Dreiser Reveals It," *Current Opinion*, LXVI (March 1919), 175-176.

Anon. "Shall It Be Dreiser? Possible Winner of This Year's Nobel Prize in Literature," *Commonweal*, XII (October 22, 1930), 622.

Anon. "Slap! Slap!" *Literary Digest*, CIX (April 11, 1931), 15-16.

Anon. "Vale," *Saturday Review of Literature*, XXIX (January 5, 1946), 16.

Anon. Valedictory," *Time*, XLVII (March 25, 1946), 102.

Anzilotti, Rolando. "Il Viaggio de Dreiser in Italia (in appendice, pagine inedite di *A Traveler at Forty*)," *Studi Americani* (Rome), XII (1966), 323-398.

———. "Theodore Dreiser: Le Fonti e il Metodo de Romanziere," *Rassegna Lucchese*, (June 1966).

Arnavon, Cyrille. "Theodore Dreiser and Painting," *American Literature*, XVII (May 1945), 113-126.

Arvin, Newton. "An American Case History," *New Republic* (August 6, 1931).

————. "Fiction Mirrors America," *Current History*, XLII (September 1934), 610-616.

Asselineau, Roger. "Theodore Dreiser's Transcendentalism," *English Studies Today*, Second Series, XI (1961), 233-246.

Atherton, Gertrude. "The Alpine School of Fiction," *Bookman*, LV (March 1922), 26-33.

Auerbach, Joseph S. "Oral Argument Against the Suppression of 'The Genius,' " *Essays and Miscellanies*, III. New York: Harper, 1922, pp. 130-168.

Austin, Mary. "Sex in American Literature," *Bookman*, LVII (June 1923), 385-393.

Avary, Mytra. "Success and Dreiser," *Colophon*, n. s., III (Autumn 1938), 598-604.

Babbitt, Irving. "The Critic and American Life," *Forum*, LCCIX (February 1928), 161-176.

Baldwin, Charles S. "Theodore Dreiser," *The Men Who Make Our Novels*. Rev. ed. New York: Dodd, Mead, 1924, pp. 141-153.

Banning, M. C. "Changing Moral Standards in Fiction," *Saturday Review of Literature*, XX (July 1, 1939), 3-4.

Barbarow, G. "Dreiser's Place on the Screen," *Hudson Review*, V (Summer 1952), 290-295.

Beach, Joseph Warren. *The Outlook for American Prose*. Chicago: University of Chicago Press, 1926, pp. 7ff.

———. "The Realist Reaction: Dreiser," *The Twentieth Century Novel*. New York: Century, 1932, pp. 320-331.

Bechhofer, Carl Eric. *The Literary Renaissance in America*. London: Heinmann, 1923, pp. 92ff.

Becker, George. "Theodore Dreiser: The Realist as Social Critic," *Twentieth Century Literature*, I (October 1955), 177-127.

Bellow, Saul. "Dreiser and the Triumph of Art," *Commentary*, XI (May 1951), 502-503.

Benét, William Rose. "Theodore Dreiser," *Encyclopaedia Britannica*, 14th edition, London, New York: Encyclopaedia Britannica, 1929, Vol. VI, p. 645.

———. "Books of the Year," *Savour of Life*. Garden City, New York: Doubleday, Doran, 1928, pp. 293-313.

Bennett, Arnold. "The Future of the American Novel," *North American Review,* CXCV (January 1912), 76-83.

Bercovici, Konrad. "Romantic Realist," *Mentor*, XVIII (May 1930), 38-41.

Berg, Ruben G. "Theodore Dreiser—Sherwood Anderson," *Moderna Amerikaner*. Stockholm: H. Geber, 1925, pp. 100-125.

Bernard, Kenneth. "The Flight of Theodore Dreiser," *University of Kansas City Review*, XXVI (June 1960), 251-259.

Berryman, John. "Though Dreiser's Imagination the Tides of Real Life Billowed," in Francis Brown, ed., *Highlights of Modern Literature*. New York: New American Library, 1954, pp. 118-123.

Berthoff, Warner, "Lives of the Americans: Theodore Dreiser," *The Ferment of Realism: American Literature 1884-1919*. New York: Free Press, 1965, pp. 235-244.

Binni, Francesco. "Dreiser olfre il Naturalismo," *Studi Americani* (Rome), XI (1965), 251-269.

Birss, John H. "Records of Theodore Dreiser: A Bibliographical Note," *Notes and Queries* CLXV (September 30, 1933), 229.

Blackmur, R. P. "The Economy of the American Writer," *Sewanee Review*, LIII (Spring 1945), 175-185.

Blackstock, Walter. "Dreiser's Dramatizations of American Success," *Florida State University Studies*, No. 14, 1954, pp. 107-130.

———. "Dreiser's Dramatizations of Art, The Artist, and the Beautiful in American Life," *Southern Quarterly*, I (1962), 63-86.

———. "The Fall and Rise of Eugene Witla: Dramatic Vision of Artistic Integrity in *The 'Genius,'* " *Language Quarterly*, V (i-ii, 1967), 15-18.

———. "Theodore Dreiser's Literary Style," *Florida State University Studies*, No. 11, 1953, pp. 95-116.

Blankenship, Russell. "Theodore Dreiser," *American Literature As an Expression of the National Mind*. New York: Holt, 1931, pp. 513ff.

Bourne, Randolph. "The Art of Theodore Dreiser," *History of a Literary Radical and Other Essays*. New York: B. W. Huebsch, 1920, pp. 195-204. Also in *Dial*, LXII (June 14, 1917), 507-509.

———. "Desire as Hero," *New Republic*, V (November 20, 1915), supp. 5-6.

———. "The Novels of Theodore Dreiser," *New Republic*, II (April 17, 1915), 78.

Bowers, Claude, "Memories of Theodore Dreiser," *My Life: The Memories of Claude Bowers*. New York: Simon and Schuster, 1962, pp. 153-172.

Boynton, Percy. "American Authors of Today: Theodore Dreiser," *English Journal*, XII (March 1923), 180-188.

———. "Theodore Dreiser," *America in Contemporary Fiction*. Chicago: University of Chicago Press, 1940, pp. 131-49.

———. "Theodore Dreiser," *Some Contemporary Americans*. Chicago: University of Chicago Press, 1924, pp. 26-144.

Brodin, Pierre. *Les Ecrivains Americains du Vingtieme Siécle*. Paris: Horizons de France, 1947.

Broe, Axel. "Theodore Dreiser," *Tilskueven*, (January 1930), 58-64.

Brooks, Van Wyck. *Letters and Leadership*. New York: Heubsch, 1918, pp. 15ff.

———. "The Literary Life in America," *Emerson and Others*. New York: Dutton, 1927, pp. 221-250.

———. "Theodore Dreiser," *The Confident Years: 1885-1915*. New York: Dutton, 1952, pp. 301-320.

———. "Theodore Dreiser," *University of Kansas City Review*, XVI (Spring 1950), 187-197.

Brown, Carrol T. "Dreiser's *Bulwark* and Philadelphia Quakerism," *Bulletin of the Friends Historical Association* (Autumn 1946).

Brown, Deming. "Sinclair Lewis and Theodore Dreiser," *Soviet Attitudes Toward American Writing*. Princeton: Princeton University Press, 1962, pp. 239-271.

Burns, Friederich. "Theodore Dreiser," *Die Amerikanische Dichung der Gegenwart*. Leipzig, Berlin: B. G. Teuhner, 1930, pp. 22-33.

Burgum, Edwin Berry. "Theodore Dreiser and the Ethics of American Life," *The Novel and the World's Dilemma*. New York: Oxford, 1947, pp. 292-301.

Burke, Kenneth. "A Decade of American Fiction," *Bookman*, LXV (August 1929), 326-329.

Butler, Gerald J. "The Quality of Emotional Greatness," *Paunch*, No. 25 (February 1966), 5-17.

Cabell, James Branch. *Some of Us*. New York: McBride, 1930, pp. 5 ff.

Cairns, William B. *A History of American Literature*. New York: Oxford University Press, 1930, pp. 488ff.

———. "Prolentarianitis," *Saturday Review of Literature*, XV (January 9, 1937), 3-4.

Calverton, Victor F. "Left-Wing Literature in America," *English Journal*, XX (December 1931), 789-798.

———. *Liberation of American Literature*. New York: Scribners, 1932, pp. 403ff.

———. "Marxism and American Literature," *Books Abroad*, VII (April 1933), 131-134.

Campbell, Charles L. "*An American Tragedy*; or Death in the Woods," *Modern Fiction Studies*, XV (Summer 1969), 251-259.

Cargill, Oscar. "Naturalists," *Intellectual America*. New York: Macmillan, 1941, pp. 107-128 ff.

Carter, John. "Dreiser Reduced Literature to Its Own Level," *New York Times Book Review*, August 9, 1925, p. 5.

Cĕder, Margarita. "Rabota Drajzer nad romanom Oplot," *Voprosy Literatury*, XI (i, 1967), 139-152.

Chamberlain, John. "Minority Report of the Novelists," *Farewell to Reform; The Rise, Life, and Decay of the Progressive Mind in America*. 2nd ed. New York: John Day, 1933.

————. "Theodore Dreiser," in Malcolm Cowley, ed. *After the Genteel Tradition*. New York: Norton, 1936, pp. 21-27.

————. "Theodore Dreiser," *New Republic*, LXXXIX (December 23, 1936), 236-238.

Chesterton, G. K. "The Skeptic as Critic," *Forum*, LXXXI (February, 1929), 65-69.

Clark, Edwin. "Self-Revelations," *Yale Review*, n. s., XX (June 1931), 856-859.

Cleaton, Irene and Allen. *Books and Battles: American Literature, 1920–1930*. Boston: Houghton, Mifflin, 1937, pp. 23 ff.

Coblentz, Stanton A. *The Literary Revolution*. New York: Frank-Marvice, 1927, pp. 151-152.

Cohen, Lester. "Theodore Dreiser: A Personal Memoir," *Discovery*, No. 4 (1954), pp. 99-126.

Combs, G. H. "Theodore Dreiser and James Branch Cabell, the Unheavenly Twins," *These Amazing Moderns*. St. Louis: Bethany, 1933, pp. 75-85.

Coursen, Herbert R. Jr. "Clyde Griffiths and the American Dream," *New Republic*, CXLV (September 4, 1961), 21-22.

Cowie, Alexander, "The New Heroine's Code for Virtue," *American Scholar*, IV (Spring 1935), 190-202.

Cowley, Malcolm. *The Literary Situation*. New York: Viking, 1954, pp. 66 ff.

———. "Naturalism in American Literature," *Evolutionary Thought in America*. New Haven: Yale University Press, 1950, pp. 300-333.

———. "Sister Carrie's Brother," *New Republic*, CXVI (May 26, 1947), 23-25.

———. "The Slow Triumph of *Sister Carrie*," *New Republic*, CXVI (June 23, 1947), 24-27.

Crawford Bruce. "Theodore Dreiser: Letter-Writing Citizen," *South Atlantic Quarterly*, LIII (April 1954), 231-237.

Croy, Homer. *Country Cured*. New York: 1943.

Cruncher, Jerry. "Epitaphs for Living Lions," *Forum*, LXXX (July 1928), 78-81.

Dana, Harry. "Russia Looks at Dreiser," *New Masses*, III (February 1929).

Davis, David B. "Dreiser and Naturalism Revisited," in Alfred Kazin and Charles Shapiro, eds. *The Stature of Theodore Dreiser*. Bloomington, Indiana: Indiana University Press, 1955, pp. 225-236.

Davis, Elmer. "The Red Peril," *Saturday Review of Literature*, VIII (April 16, 1932), 661-662.

Debouzy, Marianne. "Théodore Dreiser," *Les Langues Modernes*, VIII (April 16, 1932), 661-662.

―――. "Théodore Dreiser," *Les Langues Modernes*, LX (March 1966), 37-42.

Deegan, Dorothy Yost. *The Stereotype of the Single Woman in American Novels.* New York: Columbia University Press, 1951, pp. 49-56 ff.

Dell, Floyd. "American Fiction," *Liberator*, II (September 1919), 46-47.

―――. *Homecoming.* New York: Farrar, Rinehart, 1953, pp. 257, 268ff.

―――. "Talks with Live Authors," *Masses*, (August 1916).

De Mille, George E. "American Criticism Today," *Sewanee Review*, XXXV (July 1927), 353-358.

Drummond, Edward J., "Theodore Dreiser: Shifting Naturalism," in Harold C. Gardiner. *Fifty Years of the American Novel.* New York: Scribner, 1951, pp. 33-47.

Dudding, Griffith. "A Note Concerning Theodore Dreiser's Philosophy," *Library Chronicle* [University of Pennsylvania], XXX (Summer 1964), 36-37.

Duffus, R. L. "Dreiser," *American Mercury*, VII (January 1926), 71-76.

Dynamov, S. "Theodore Dreiser Continues the Struggle," *International Literature*, Nos. 2-3, 1932, pp. 112-115.

Earnest, Ernest. "The American Ariel," *South Atlantic Quarterly*, LXV (Spring 1966), 192-200.

Eastman, Max. "Is the Novel at a Dead End?" *The Literary Mind.* New York: Scribner, 1931, pp. 225-237.

Edgar, Pelham, "American Realism, Sex, and Theodore Dreiser," *The Art of the Novel*. New York: Macmillan, 1933, pp. 244-254.

Eisenstein, Sergei. "Un Projet: l'adaptation de *An American Tragedy*," *La Revue des Letters Modernes*, V (1958), 88-97.

Elias, Robert H. "Theodore Dreiser," in Jackson R. Bryer, ed. *Fifteen Modern American Authors: A Survey of Research and Criticism*. Durham: Duke University Press, 1969, pp. 101-138.

―――. "The Library's Dreiser Collection," *Library Chronicle* [University of Pennsylvania], XVII (Fall 1950), 78-80.

Ernst, Morris. *The the Pure . . . A Study in Obscenity and the Censor*. New York: Viking, 1928, pp. 7 ff.

Erskine, John. "American Business in the American Novel," *Bookman*, LXXIII (July 1931), 449-457.

Fadiman, Clifton. "Dreiser and the American Dream," *Nation*, CXXXV (October 19, 1932), 364-365.

Farrell, James T. "Dreiser," *New York Times Book Review*, January 8, 1956, p. 22.

―――. "Dreiser's *Sister Carrie*," *The League of Frightened Philistines*. New York: Vangard, 1945, pp. 12-19.

―――. "A Literary Behemoth Against the Backdrop of His Era," *New York Times Book Review*, July 4, 1943, p. 3.

―――. "Social Themes in American Realism," *English Journal*, XXXV (June 1946), 309-314.

―――. "Some Aspects of Dreiser's Fiction," *New York Times Book Review*, April 29, 1945, p. 7; May 6, 1945, p. 6.

———. "Some Correspondence with Theodore Dreiser," *General Magazine and Historical Chronicle* [University of Pennsylvania], LIII (Summer 1951), 237-252.

———. "Theodore Dreiser," *Chicago Review*, I (Summer 1946), 127-144.

———. "Theodore Dreiser: in Memoriam," *Saturday Review of Literature*, XXIX (January 12, 1946), 15-17, 27-28.

Fast, Howard, "Dreiser's Short Stories," *New Masses*, LX (September 3, 1946), 11-12.

———. "He Knew the People," *Sunday Worker*, December 30, 1945.

Feld, Rose C. "Interview with Dreiser," *New York Times Book Review*, December 23, 1923, pp. 6-7.

Fiedler, Leslie A. *Love and Death in the American Novel*, rev. ed. New York: Stein and Day, 1966, pp. 247-255.

Field, Louise M. "American Novelists Against the Nation," *North American Review*, CCXXXV (June 1933), 552-560.

Filler, Louis. "Sense, Sentimentality, and Theodore Dreiser," *Salamagundi*, I (1966), 90-97.

———. "A Tale of Two Authors: Theodore Dreiser and David Graham Phillips," in David B. Browne, Donald M. Winkleman, and Allen Hayman, eds., *New Voices in American Studies*. Lafayette, Indiana: Purdue University Press, 1966, pp. 35-48.

Fischer, Louis. "Russia Adopts Dreiser," *New York Herald Tribune Books*, October 4, 1931.

Flanagan, John T. "Dreiser's Style in *An American Tragedy*," *Texas Studies in Language and Literature*, VII (Autumn 1965), 285-294.

————. "Theodore Dreiser in Retrospect, *Southwest Review*, XXVI (Autumn 1946), 905-911.

————. "Theodore Dreiser's Chicago," *Revue des Langues Vivantes*, XXXII (1966), 131-144.

Flint, R. W. "Dreiser: The Press of Life," *Nation*, CLXXXIV (April 27, 1957), 371-373.

Follett, Helen and Wilson. "The Younger Generation," *Some Modern Novelists, Appreciations and Estimates*. New York: Holt, 1948, pp. 350-352.

Ford, Corey [John Riddell]. "Blue-print for Another American Tragedy," *Meaning No Offense*. New York: John Day, 1927, pp. 65-72.

————. "Dawn Jawn," *In the Worst Possible Taste*. New York: Scribner, 1932, pp. 17-27.

Ford, Ford Madox. "Dreiser," *Portraits From Life*. Boston: Houghton, Mifflin, 1937, pp. 164-182. Also appeared in part in *American Mercury*, XL (April 1937), 488-96.

Frank, Waldo. "Chicago," *Our America*. New York: Boni and Liveright, 1919, pp. 117-146.

————. "Our Arts: The Re-Discovery of America: XII," *New Republic*, LIV (May 9, 1928), 343-347.

Franz, Eleanor W. "The Tragedy of the 'North Woods,' " *New York Folklore Quarterly*, IV (Summer 1948), 85-96.

Freedman, William A. "A Look at Dreiser as Artist: The Motif of Circularity in *Sister Carrie*," *Modern Fiction Studies*, VIII (Winter 1962/1963), 384-392.

Friede, Donald. *The Mechanical Angel: His Adventures and Enterprises in the Glittering 1920's*. New York: Knopf, 1948, pp. 22ff.

Friedrich, Gerhard. "A Major Influence on Theodore Dreiser's *The Bulwark,*" *American Literature*, XXIX (May 1957), 180-193.

———. "Theodore Dreiser's Debt to Woman's Journal," *American Quarterly*, VII (Winter 1955), 385-392.

Gale, Zona. "Period Realism," *Yale Review*, n. s., XVII (Autumn 1933), 111-124.

Garnett, Edward. "American Criticism and Fiction." *Friday Nights*. New York: Knopf, 1922, pp. 227-235.

Geismar, Maxwell. "Dreiser and the Dark Texture of Life," *American Scholar*, XXII (Spring 1952), 215-221.

———. "Theodore Dreiser: The Double Soul," *Rebels and Ancestors: The American Novel, 1890–1915*. Boston: Houghton, Mifflin, 1953, pp. 287-379.

———. "Jezebel on the Loop," *Saturday Review of Literature*, XXXVI (July 4, 1953), 12.

Gelfant, Blanche H. "Theodore Dreiser: the Portrait Novel," *The American City Novel*. Norman, Oklahoma: University of Oklahoma Press, 1954, pp. 42-94.

Gibbs, Donald. "Dreiser the Dull," *Forum*, LXXVIII (December 1927), 155-56.

Gilkes, Martin. "Discovering Dreiser," *New Adelphi*, II (December 1928), 178-218.

Glicksberg, Charles I. "Fiction and Philosophy," *Arizona Quarterly*, XIII (Spring 1947), 5-17.

———. "Literature and Science: A Study in Conflict," *Science Monthly*, LIX (December 1944), 467-472.

————. "Proletarian Fiction in the United States," *Dalhousie Review*, XVII (April 1937), 22-32.

————. "Two Decades of Literary Criticism," *Dalhousie Review*, XVI (July 1936), 229-242.

Gold, Michael. "The Dreiser I Knew," *The Mike Gold Reader*, ed. by Samuel Sillen. New York: 1954.

Goldberg, Isaac. *The Man Mencken: A Biographical and Critical Survey*. New York: Simon and Schuster, 1924, pp. 14ff.

Goodfellow, Donald M. "Theodore Dreiser and The American Dream," in William M. Schulte *et al.*, *Six Novelists: Sendhal, Dostoevski, Tolstoy, Hardy, Dreiser, and Proust*. Pittsburgh: Carnegie Institute of Technology Press, 1959, pp. 145-156.

Garbo, Carl H. *The Technique of the Novel*. New York: Scribner, 1928, pp. 258 ff.

Grana, Cianni. "La Rinascita del Naturalismo in Americana: Anderson and Dreiser," *Fiera Letteria*, No. 3, p. 4.

Grattan, C. Hartley. "Upton Sinclair on Current Literature," *Bookman*, LXXVI (April 1932), 61-64.

Grebstein, Sheldon N. "Dreiser's Victorian Vamp," *Midcontinent American Studies Journal*, IV (1963), 3-12.

————. "*An American Tragedy*: Theme and Structure," in Richard Langford, and W. E. Taylor, eds. The *Twenties, Poetry and Prose: Twenty Critical Essays*. Deland, Florida: Everett Edwards Press, 1966, pp. 62-66.

Green, Elizabeth and Paul. "Theodore Dreiser," *Contemporary American Literature*, Chapel Hill, N. C.: University of North Carolina Press, 1925, pp. 12-15.

Griffin, Ernest G. "Sympathetic Materialism: A Rereading of Theodore Dreiser," *Humanities Association Bulletin,* XX (i, 1969), 59-68.

Hackett, Francis. Horizons: "Correctness," *A Book of Criticism.* New York: B. W. Huebsh, 1919, pp. 13-20.

Hakutani, Yoshinobu. "Dreiser and French Realism," *Texas Studies in Language and Literature,* VI (Summer 1964), 200-212.

———. "Sinclair Lewis and Dreiser: A Study in Continuity and Development," *Discourse,* VII (Summer 1964), 254-276.

———. "*Sister Carrie* and the Problem of Literary Naturalism," *Twentieth Century Literature,* XIII (April 1967), 3-17.

Haley, Carmen O'Neill. "The Dreisers," *Commonweal,* XVIII (July 7, 1933), 265-267.

Halleck, Rubin P. "Theodore Dreiser 1871," *The Romance of American Literature.* New York: American Book, 1934, pp. 309-314.

Handy, William J. "A Re-examination of Dreiser's *Sister Carrie,*" *Texas Studies in Language and Literature,* I (Autumn 1959), 380-393.

Hansen, Erik A. "Theodore Dreiser," in Sven M. Kristensen, ed. *Fremmede Digtere i detao. Århundrede.* Copenhagen: G. E. C. Gad, 1967, Vol. I, pp. 217-228.

Hansen, Harry. "Fashions in Fiction," *Forum,* LXXXIX (March 1933), 1152-1155.

Hapgood, Hutchins. "Is Dreiser Anti-Semitic?" *Nation,* CXL (April 17, 1935), 436-438. Further discussion in *Nation,* CXL (May 15, 1935), 572-573.

————. *A Victorian in the Modern World*. New York: Harcourt, Brace, 1939, pp. 266ff.

Hardwick, Elizabeth. "Fiction Chronicle," *Partisan Review*, XV (January 1948), 108-117.

Harris, Frank. "Theodore Dreiser," *Contemporary Portraits*: *Second Series*. New York: the Author, 1919, pp. 81-106.

Hartwick, Harry. "Hindenburg of the Novel," *The Foreground of American Fiction*. New York: American Book Company, 1934, pp. 85-110 ff.

Hatcher, Harlan. *Creating the Modern American Novel*. New York: Farrar and Rinehart, 1935, pp. 10ff.

Hazard, Lucy L. "Theodore Dreiser: Cowperwood, the Creature of Chemistry," *The Frontier in American Literature*. New York: Crowell, 1927, pp. 235-242.

Hazlitt, Henry. "All Too Humanist," *Nation*, CXXX (February 12, 1930), 181-182.

————. "Literature as Propaganda," *Saturday Review of Literature*, XX (September 16, 1937), 13-15.

————. "Our Greatest Authors: How Great Are They?" *Forum*, LXXXVIII (October 1932), 245-250.

Hedges, M. H. "Mr. Dreiser," *Dial*, LXII (April 19, 1917), 343.

Hellesnes, Nils. "Theodore Dreiser," *Syn Og Segn* (March 1947).

Herrmann, Eva. *On Parade*. New York: Coward-McCann, 1929, pp. 46-49.

Heustin, Dustin. "Theodore Dreiser: Naturalist or Theist," *Brigham Young University Studies*, III (Winter 1961), 41-49.

Hicks, Granville. *The Great Tradition*. New York: Macmillan, 1933, pp. 227-232 ff.

———. "The Gutter—and Then What," *Forum*, LXXX (December 1928), 801-810.

———. "Literature and Revolution," *English Journal*, XXIV (March 1935), 219-223.

———. "Theodore Dreiser," *American Mercury*, LXII (June 1946), 751-756.

———. "The Twenties in American Literature," *Nation*, CXXX (February 12, 1930), 183-185.

Hodgins, Francis Jr. "The Dreiser Letters," *Journal of English and Germanic Philology*, LIX (October 1960), 714-720.

Hoffman, Frederick J. *The Modern Novel in America*. Chicago: Regnery, 1951, pp. 40-51 ff.

———. *The Mortal No*. Princeton: Princeton University Press, 1964, pp. 194-201.

———. "The Scene of Violence: Dostoevsky and Dreiser," *Modern Fiction Studies*, VI (Summer 1960), 91-105.

Howard, Leon. *Literature and the American Tradition*. Garden City, New Jersey: Doubleday, 1966, pp. 227ff.

Howe, Irving. "The Stature of Theodore Dreiser," *New Republic*, CLI (July 25, 1964), 19-21.

———. "Dreiser and Tragedy," *New Republic*, CLI (August 22, 1964), 25-28.

Hunt, E. L. "The Social Interpretation of Literature," *English Journal*, College Edition, XXIV (March 1935), 214 ff.

Huth, J. F., Jr. "Dreiser and *Success*: An Additional Note," *Colophon*, I (Winter 1938), 406-410. See also Avary above.

―――. "Theodore Dreiser, Success Monger," *Colophon*, n.s., III (Winter 1938), 120-133.

―――. "Theodore Dreiser: 'The Prophet,' " *American Literature*, IX (May 1937), 347-354.

Johns, Orrick. *Time of Our Lives*. New York: Stackpole, 1937, pp. 216, 326ff.

Jones, Howard Mumford. "Dreiser Reconsidered," *Atlantic Monthly*, CLXXVII (May 1946), 162-170.

―――. "Theodore Dreiser—A Pioneer Whose Fame Is Secure," *New York Times Book Review*, January 13, 1946, p. 1.

Josephson, Matthew. "Dreiser, Reluctant, In the Films," *New Republic*, LXVIII (August 19, 1931), 21-22.

Karsner, David. "Theodore Dreiser," *Sixteen Authors to One*. New York: Lewis Copeland, 1928, pp. 3-24.

Katope, Christpher G. "*Sister Carrie* and Spencer's *First Principles*," *American Literature*, XLI (March 1969), 64-75.

Katz, Joseph. "Theodore Dreiser at Indiana University," *Notes and Queries*, n.s., XIII (March 1966), 100-101.

―――. "Theodore Dreiser: Enter Chicago, Hope, and Walt Whitman," *Walt Whitman Review*, XIV (December 1968), 169-171.

Kaun, Alexander S. "Choleric Comments," *Little Review*, II (November 1915), 20-23.

Kazin, Alfred. "General Introduction," *Sister Carrie*. New York: Dell, 1960. Same introduction appears in other Dell editions of Dreiser's works with the exception of *Jennie Gerhardt*.

————. "Dreiser," *The Inmost Leaf*. New York: Harcourt, Brace & World, 1955, pp. 236-241.

————. "Introduction," *Jennie Gerhardt*. New York: Dell, 1963.

————. "Lady and the Tiger," *Virginia Quarterly Review*, XVII (January 1941), 111-119.

————. "Two Educations: Edith Wharton and Theodore Dreiser," *On Native Grounds*. New York: Reynal and Hitchcock, 1942, pp. 73-90.

Kelly, C. "American Victory or Tragedy; Dreiser versus Ulysses S. Grant," *National Republic*, XVII (March, April 1930), 16-17; 28-29.

Kern, Alexander, "Dreiser's Difficult Beauty," *Western Review*, XVI (Winter 1952), 129-132.

Khaindrava, L. "Problema zhenshchiny v Romanakh Draizera," *Literaturnaya Gruziya* [Tbilisi], III (1967), 90-95.

————. "Teodore Draizero Sud'be zhenshchiny v Kapitalisticheskam mire," *Trudy Tbiliskogo Pedagogicheskogo Instituta*, XIX (1967), 233-247.

Kirk, C. M. "The Marxist Doctrine in Literature," *English Journal*, College Edition, XXIV (March 1935), 209-214.

Knight, Grant C. *The Novel in English*. New York: R. R. Smith, 1931, pp. 338-346.

Kramer, Dale. "Dreiser, Masks of the Monster and Hero," *Chicago Renaissance*. New York: Appleton-Century, 1966, pp. 128-139.

Krim, Seymour. "Dreiser and His Critics," *Commonweal*, LXIV (June 1, 1956), 229-231.

Krutch, Joseph Wood. "Dreiser Simplified," *Nation*, CXLII (April 1, 1936), 427-429.

———. "Literature and Propaganda," *English Journal*, XXII (December 1933), 793-802.

Krylova, L. A. "Esteticheskii poisk T. Draizera posk Oktyabr-'skoi Revolyutsii," *Nekotorye voprosy Istorii i Teorii Estetiki* (Sbornik aspirantskikh rabot) Moskow, 1967, pp. 15-28.

Kunitz, Stanley, Jr. "Dreiser, Theodore," *Twentieth Century Authors*. New York: Wilson, 1931, pp. 378-379.

Kwiat, Joseph J. "Dreiser and the Graphic Artist," *American Quarterly*, III (Summer 1951), 127-141.

———. "Dreiser's *The 'Genius'* and Everett Shin, 'The Ash Can Painter,' " *PMLA*, LXVII (March 1952), 15-31.

———. "The Newspaper Experience: Crane, Norris, and Dreiser," *Nineteenth-Century Fiction*, VIII (September 1953), 99-117.

———. "Theodore Dreiser: The Winter and Early Twentieth Century American Society," *Sprache und Literature Englands und Amerikas: Lehrganysvortrage der Akademie Comburg*, II (1956), 135-150.

Lane, Lauriat, Jr. "The Double in *An American Tragedy*," *Modern Fiction Studies*, XII (Summer 1966), 213-20.

Lawson, John Howard. "Dreiser: 20th Century Titan," *Sunday Worker*, February 3, 1946, p. 4.

Le Verrier, Charles. "Un Grand Romancier Americain: Theodore Dreiser," *Revue Hebdomadaire*, 2nd series, 42e Annee (January 21, 1933), 280-295.

Lehan, Richard. "Dreiser's *An American Tragedy*: A Critical Study," *College English*, XXV (December 1963), 187-193.

Leisy, Ernest E. *American Literature: An Interpretative Survey*. New York: Crowell, 1929.

Lengel, William C. "The 'Genius' Himself," *Esquire*, X (September 1938), 55, 120, 124, 126.

Leonard, Neil. "Theodore Dreiser and the Film," *Film Heritage* (Fall 1966).

Lerner, Max. "On Dreiser," *Actions and Passions*. New York: Simon and Schuster, 1949, pp. 43-46.

Levin, Harry. "What is Realism?" *Comparative Literature*, III (Summer 1951), 193-199.

Levinson, Andrei Y. "Avant-Propos" in Dreiser *Un Tragedie Americains*, ed. Victor Llona. Paris: Univers, 1929, pp. 7-16.

Lewis, Sinclair. "Nobel Prize Speech of 1930," *New York Times*, December 13, 1930, p. 12.

Lewis, Wyndham. "The Propagandist in Fiction," *Current History*, XL (August, 1934), 567-572.

Lewisohn, Ludwig. "Culture and Barbarism," *Cities and Men*. New York: Harper Bros., 1927, pp. 2-18.

———. *Expression in America*. New York: Harper, 1932, pp. 473 ff.

———. "Portrait of an Artist," *Nation*, CXVI (April 4, 1923), 394.

Loggins, Vernon. "Dominant Primordial," *I Hear America . . . Literature in the United States Since 1900*. New York: Crowell, 1937, pp. 125-134 ff.

Lombardo, Agostino. "Lettere Di Dreiser," *La Rivera del Vero: Saggi sulla Tradizione Letteraria Americana*. Rome: Ed. di Storia e Letteratur, 1961, pp. 309-315.

Long, Robert E. "Dreiser and Frederic: The Upstate New York Exile of Dick Diver," *Fitzgerald Newsletter*, No. 37 (Winter 1967), 1-2.

Lord, David. "Dreiser Today," *Prairie Schooner*, XV (Winter 1941), 230-237.

Luccock, H. E. *Contemporary American Literature and Religion*. Chicago: Willett, Clark, 1934, pp. 4 ff.

Ludlow, Francis. "Plodding Crusader," *College English*, VII (October 1946), 1-7.

Lydenburg, John. "Theodore Dreiser: Ishmael in the Jungle," *Monthly Review*, VII (August 1954), 124-136.

Lynn, Kenneth S. "Theodore Dreiser: The Man of Ice," *The Dream of Success*. Boston: Little, Brown, 1955, pp. 13-75.

Lyons, Eugene. *The Red Decade; The Stalinist Penetration of America*. Indianapolis: Bobbs-Merrill, 1941, pp. 80 ff.

McAfee, Helen. "The Literature of Dilissusion," *Atlantic Monthly*, CXXXII (August 1923), 225-234.

McCole, John. "Theodore Dreiser and The Rise of American Realism," *Lucifer at Large*. London, New York: Longmans, Green, 1937, pp. 17-54.

―――. "The Tragedy of Theodore Dreiser," *Catholic World*, CXXXII (October 1930), 1-7.

MacCollough, Martin (pseud.) [Samuel W. Tait, Jr.]. *Letters on Contemporary American Authors*. Boston: Four Seas Co., 1921, pp. 81-87 ff.

McDonald, Edward D. "Dreiser Before Sister Carrie," *Bookman*, LXVII (June 1928), 369-374.

Manchester, William. *Disturber of the Peace: The Life of H. L. Mencken*. New York: Harper, 1951, pp. 36 ff.

Marble, Annie R. "Revolt and Escape," *A Study of the Modern Novel, British and American, Since 1900*. New York: Appleton, 1928, pp. 366-372.

Markels, Julian. "Dreiser and the Plotting of Inarticulate Experience," *Massachusetts Review*, II (1961), 431-448.

Marquis, Don. "205 Words," *Saturday Review of Literature*, IX (October 15, 1932), 174.

Martin, Jay. "The Visible and Invisible Cities," *Harvests of Change*. Englewood Cliffs, New Jersey: Prentice-Hall, 1967, pp. 252-263.

Masters, Edgar Lee. *Across Spoon River*. New York: Farrar & Rinehart, 1936, pp. 145 ff.

Matthiessen, F. O. "Dreiser's Politics," *Tomorrow*, X (January 1951), 10-17.

―――. "Of Crime and Punishment," *Monthly Review*, II (October 1950), 189-204.

Maurice, Arthur B. "Makers of Modern American Fiction (Men)," *Mentor*, VI (September 1, 1918), 1-11.

Mayfield, Sara. "Another Fitzgerald Myth Exploded by Mencken," *Fitzgerald Newsletter*, No. 32 (Winter 1966), 1.

Mazets'kii, G. "Okrilenii Zhovtnem: Do Pitannya pro Evolyutsiyu Evitoglyodii i Tvorchosti Teodora Draizera," *Radyans'ske Literaturozhavstvo* [Kiev], X (1967), 19-25.

Mencken, H. L. "The American Novel," *Prejudices: Fourth Series*. New York: Knopf, 1924, pp. 279-293.

––––––. "The Creed of a Novelist," *Smart Set*, L (October 1916), 138-143.

––––––. "The Dreiser Bugaboo," *The Seven Arts*, II (August 1917), 507-517.

––––––. "Footnote on Criticism," *Prejudices: Third Series*. New York: Knopf, 1922, pp. 84-104.

––––––. "That Was New York: The Life of an Artist," *New Yorker*, XXIV (April 17, 1948), 43-57.

––––––. "Theodore Dreiser," *A Book of Prefaces*. New York: Knopf, 1917, pp. 67-148. Also in Edmund Wilson, ed., *The Shock of Recognition*. Garden City, N. J.: Doubleday, 1943, pp. 1160-1208.

Meyer, George W. "The Original Social Purpose of the Naturalistic Novel," *Sewanee Review*, L (October–December 1942), 563-570.

Michaud, Regis. "Theodore Dreiser," *Panorama de la Littera-ture Americaine Contemporaine*. Paris: Kra, 1928, pp. 165-170.

————. *Le roman americain d'aujourd'hui*. Paris: Boivin, 1926. Translated as *The American Novel of Today*. Boston: Little Brown, 1928, pp. 71-127.

Miller, Henry. *The Books in My Life*. London: P. Owens, 1952, pp. 218-221.

Millgate, Michael. "Theodore Dreiser," *American Social Fiction; James to Cozzens*. Edinburgh: Oliver and Boyd; New York: Barnes and Noble, 1964, pp. 67-86.

————. "Theodore Dreiser and the American Financier," *Studi Americani*, VII (1961), 133-145.

Moers, Ellen. "The Finesse of Dreiser," *American Scholar*, XXXIII (Winter 1963), 109-114.

————. "New Light on Dreiser in the 1890's," *Columbia Library Columns*, XV (May 1966), 10-24.

Mookerjee, R. N. "The Social Content of *Jennie Gerhardt*," in Rameshwar Gupta, ed. *Bannasthali Patrika*, XI (July 1968), 31-36.

Moore, H. T. "The American Novel Today," *London Mercury*, XXXI (March 1935), 109-114.

Mordell, Albert. "My Relations with Theodore Dreiser," *Critic Guide*, V (March 1951), 1-7.

More, Paul Elmer. "Modern Currents in American Literature," *The Demon of the Absolute*. Princeton: Princeton University Press, 1928, pp. 53-76.

————. "A Revival of Humanism," *Bookman*, LXXI (March 1930), 1-11.

Morgan, H. Wayne. *American Writers in Rebellion from Mark Twain to Dreiser*. New York: Hill and Wang, 1965.

Morris, Lloyd R. "Puzzled Iconoclast," *Postscript to Yesterday.* New York: Random House, 1947, pp. 121-130.

Muller, Herbert J. "Impressionism and Fiction," *American Scholar*, VII (Summer 1930), 355-367.

———. *Modern Fiction: A Study of Values.* New York: Funk and Wagnalls, 1937, pp. 22 ff.

———. "The New Psychology in Old Fiction," *Saturday Review of Literature*, XVI (August 21, 1937), 3-4.

Mumford, Lewis. "The Shadow of the Muckrake," *The Golden Day.* New York: Boni and Liveright, 1926, pp. 125 ff.

Munson, Gorham B. "Motivation of Theodore Dreiser," *Destinations: A Canvass of American Literature since 1900.* New York: J. H. Sears, 1928, pp. 41-56.

———. "Our Post-War Novel," *Bookman*, LXXIV (October 1931), 141-144.

Nagahara, Makoto. "Dreiser at the Turn of the Century—*Sister Carrie*," *Ritsumeikan Bungaki* (February 1963).

Nathan, George Jean. "Editorial Conference," The *American Spectator Yearbook.* New York: Stokes, 1934, pp. 346-359.

———. *The Intimate Notebooks of George Jean Nathan.* New York: Knopf, 1932, pp. 38-53.

———. "Memories of Fitzgerald, Lewis, and Dreiser," *Esquire*, L (October 1958), 148-154.

———. "Three Friends: Lewis, O'Neill, Dreiser," Carl Van Doren ed., *The Borzoi Reader.* New York: Knopf, 1936, pp. 579-615.

Noble, David W. "Dreiser and Veblen and the Literature of Cultural Change," in Joseph Kwiat, and M. Turpie, *Studies in American Culture: Dominant Ideas and Images.* Minneapolis: University of Minnesota Press, 1960, pp. 139-52.

————. *The Eternal Adam and the New World Garden.* New York: Braziller, pp. 124-32.

North, Sterling. "Dreiser's Last Testament," *New York Post,* March 21, 1946.

Notman, Otis. "Talks with Four Novelists; Mr. Dreiser," *New York Times,* June 15, 1907, p. 393.

Nugent, Walter. "Carter H. Harrison and Dreiser's 'Walden Lucas,' " *Newberry Library Bulletin,* VI (September 1966), 222-230.

O'Brien, Edward J. *The Advance of the American Short Story.* New York: Dodd, Mead, 1923, pp. 222 ff.

Overton, Grant M. "Dreiser," *An Hour of the American Novel.* Philadelphia: Lippincott, 1929, pp. 104-108.

Parrington, Vernon L. "The Development of Realism," in Norman Forerster, ed. *The Reinterpretation of American Literature.* New York: Harcourt Brace, 1928, pp. 139-159.

————. "Theodore Dreiser: Chief of American Naturalists," *Main Currents of American Thought.* Vol. III. New York: Harcourt, Brace, 1930, pp. 334-359.

Pattee, Fred L. "Theodore Dreiser," *The New American Literature,* 1890-1930. New York: Century, 1930, pp. 180-192 ff.

Pavese, Cesare. "Dreiser e la sua Battaglia Sociale," *La Cultura,* XII (April–June 1933), 431-437.

84

Phillips, William L. "The Imagery of Dreiser's Novels,"
PMLA, LXXVIII (December 1963), 572-585.

Pizer, Donald. "Nineteenth Century American Naturalism:
An Essay in Definition," *Bucknell Review*, XIII (December
1965), 1-18.

——. *Realism and Naturalism in Nineteenth Century
American Literature*. Carbondale, Ill.: Southern Illinois
University Press, 1966.

——. "Theodore Dreiser's 'Nigger Jeff': The Development of
an Aesthetic," *American Literature*, XLI (1969),
331-341.

Poirier, Ricard. *A World Elsewhere: The Place of Style in
American Literature*. New York: Oxford University Press,
1966, pp. 235-252.

Posselt, Erich. "Statements of Belife," *Bookman*, LXVIII (September, 1928), 25-27, 204-207.

Powys, John Cowper. *Autobiography*. New York: Simon and
Schuster, 1934, pp. 411 ff.

——. *One Hundred Best Books*. New York: G. A. Shaw,
1916, p. 29.

Powys, Llewelyn. "Good Friends," *The Verdict of Bridlegoose*.
New York: Harcourt, Brace, 1926, pp. 40 ff.

Preston, John Hyde. "True Style," *Saturday Review of Literature*, II (May 22, 1926), 814.

——. "Theodore Dreiser," *The Man in the Mirror: William
Marion Reedy and His Magazine*. Cambridge: Harvard
University Press, 1963, pp. 120-131 ff.

Purdy, Strother B. "*An American Tragedy* and *L'Etranger*,"
Comparative Literature, XIX (1967), 252-268.

Putzel, Max. "Dreiser, Reedy, and "De Maupassant, Junior,' "
    American Literature, XXXIII (January 1962), 466-484.

Quinn, Arthur H. *American Fiction*. New York, London:
    Appleton-Century, 1936, pp 642-652 ff.

Rahv, Phillip. "On the Decline of Naturalism," *Partisan Review*
    (November–December, 1942), 483-493.

———. "Proletarian Literature: A Political Autopsy," *Southern
    Review*, IV (January 1939), 616-628.

Rapin, Rene. "Dreiser's *Jennie Gerhardt*, Chapter LXII,"
    Explicator, XIV (May 1956), item 54.

Rascoe, Burton. *A Bookman's Daybook*, ed. C. Hartley Grattan.
    New York: Liveright, 1929, pp. 53 ff.

———. "Does Dreiser's Final Novel Reveal Spiritual Creed?"
    Chicago Tribune, March 24, 1946.

———. *We were Interrupted*. Garden City: Doubleday, 1947,
    pp. 146 ff.

———. "Theodore Dreiser," *Prometheans, Ancient and
    Modern*. New York, London: Putnam's 1933, pp. 241-269.

Rice, Diana. "Terrible Typewriter on Parnassus," *New York
    Times Magazine*, April 27, 1924, p. 11.

Richards, Grant. *Author Hunting by an Old Literary Sports-
    man*. London: Hamish Hamilton; New York:
    Coward-McCann, 1934, pp. 170-187, 188-206.

Richman, Sidney. "Theodore Dreiser's *The Bulwark*: A Final
    Resolution," *American Literature*, XXXIV (May 1962),
    229-245.

Rolfe, Edwin. "Theodore Dreiser," *Poetry*, LXVIII (June
    1946), 134-136.

Rolo, Charles J. "Dreiser's America," *Tomorrow*, VII (February 1948), 55-59.

Rosenberg, Bernard. "Mr. Trilling, Theodore Dreiser (and Life in the U.S.)," *Dissent*, II (Spring 1955), 171-178.

Ross, Woodburn O. "Concerning Dreiser's Mind," *American Literature*, XVIII (November 1946), 233-243.

Rubenstein, Annette. "A Pillar of Society," *New Masses*, LIX (April 30, 1946), 23-24.

Salzman, Jack. "The Critical Recognition of *Sister Carrie*: 1900–1907," *Journal of American Studies*, III (1969), 123-133.

————. "Dreiser and Ade: A Note on the Text of *Sister Carrie*," *American Literature*, XL (January 1969), 544-548.

————. "The Publication of *Sister Carrie*: Fact and Fiction," *Library Chronicle* [University of Pennsylvania], XXXIII (1967), 119-133.

Sampson, Ashley. "Religion in Modern Literature," *Contemporary Review*, CXLVII (April 1935), 462-470.

Samuels, Charles T. "Mr. Trilling, Mr. Warren, and *An American Tragedy*," *Yale Review*, LIII (Summer 1964), 629-640.

Schelling, F. E. "The Greatest Play Since Shakespeare," *Appraisements and Asperities As To Some Contemporary Writers*. Philadelphia: Lippincott, 1922, pp. 120-125.

Schneider, Isidor. "Theodore Dreiser," *Saturday Review of Literature*, X (March 10, 1934), 533-535.

Schneider, Robert W. "Theodore Dreiser: the Cry of Despair." *Five Novelists of the Progressive Era*. New York: Columbia University Press, 1965, pp. 153-204.

Schriftgiesser, K. "Boston Stays Pure," *New Republic*, LVIII (May 8, 1929), 327-329.

Schyberg, Frederik. *Moderne Americansk Litteratur, 1900–1930*. Copenhagen: Gyldendaske, 1930, pp. 38-45.

Scott, Kenneth W. "Did Dreiser Cut Up Jack Harkaway?" *Markham Review*, No. 2 (May 1968), 1-4.

Seaver, Edwin. "Theodore Dreiser and the American Novel," *New Masses*, I (May 1926), 24.

Sebastyen, Karl. "Theodore Dreiser at Home," *Living Age*, CCCXXXIX (December 1930), 375-378.

Shafer, Robert. "*An American Tragedy*: A Humanistic Demurrer," in Norman Foerster, ed., *Humanism and America*. New York: Farrar and Rinehart, 1930.

Shapiro, Charles K. "Jennie Gerhardt: The American Family and The American Dream," in *Twelve Original Essays on Great American Novels*. Detroit: Wayne State University Press, 1958, pp. 177-195.

Sherman, Stuart P. "Mr. Dreiser in Tragic Realism," *The Main Stream*. New York: Scribner, 1927, pp. 134-144.

———. "The Naturalism of Mr. Dreiser," *Nation*, CI (December 2, 1915), 148-150.

Sherwood, Margaret. "Characters in Recent Fiction," *Atlantic Monthly*, CIX (May 1912), 672-684.

Sillen, Samuel. "Dreiser's J'Accuse," *New Masses*, XXXVIII (January 28, 1941), 24-26.

———. "His Art Led Him To Communism," *Daily Worker*, XXII (December 31, 1945), 4, 9.

Simon, Jean. *Le Roman Americain au XXe Siecle*. Paris: Boivin, 1950.

Simpson, Claude M., Jr. "*Sister Carrie* Reconsidered," *Southwest Review*, XLIV (Winter 1959), 44-53.

————. "Theodore Dreiser, *Sister Carrie*," in Wallace Stegner, ed., *The American Novel from James Fenimore Cooper to William Faulkner*. New York: Basic Books, 1965, pp. 106-116.

Smith, Bernard. *Forces in American Criticism*. New York: Harcourt, Brace, 1939, pp. 159 ff.

Smith, Edward H. "Dreiser After 20 Years," *Bookman*, LIII (March 1921), 27-34.

Smith, Lewis W. *Current Reviews*. New York: Holt, 1926, pp. 203-212.

Smith, R. W. "Portrait of an American: the National Character in Fiction," *Southwest Review*, XXI (April 1936), 245-260.

Snell, George. "Theodore Dreiser: Philosopher," *The Shapers of American Fiction, 1708-1947*. New York: Holt, 1947, pp. 233-245 ff.

Spiller, Robert E. "Alchemy of Literature," *The Third Dimension*. New York: 1965.

————. "Dreiser as Master Craftsman," *Saturday Review of Literature*, XXIX (March 23, 1946), 23.

————. "Second Renaissance: Dreiser, Frost," *The Cycle of American Literature*. New York: Macmillan, 1955, pp. 211-42.

————. "Theodore Dreiser," *Literary History of the United States*. New York: Macmillan, 1948, Vol. II, pp. 1197-1207.

Stalnaker, J. M. and Fred Eggan. "American Novelists Ranked: A Psychological Study," *English Journal,* XVIII (April, 1929), 295-307.

Stark, Harold. "The Genius," *People You Know.* New York: Boni and Liveright, 1924, pp. 68-70.

Steadman, R. W. "A Critique of Proletarian Literature," *North American Review,* CCXLVII (Spring 1939), 142-152.

Steinbrecher, George. "Inaccurate Accounts of *Sister Carrie,*" *American Literature,* XXIII (January 1952), 490-493.

Stevens, Bennett. "The Gnats and Dreiser," *New Masses,* (May 1932).

Stewart, Randall. *American Literature and Christian Doctrine.* Baton Rouge: Louisiana State University, 1908, pp. 113 ff.

————. "Dreiser and the Naturalistic Heresy," *Virginia Quarterly Review,* XXXIV (Winter 1958), 100-116.

Stoddard, Donald R. "Mencken and Dreiser: An Exchange of Roles," *Library Chronicle* [University of Pennsylvania], XXXII (Winter 1966), 117-136.

Stovall, Floyd. "From Idealism to Naturalism," *American Idealism.* Norman, Oklahoma: University of Oklahoma Press, 1943, pp. 133 ff.

Strauss, Harold. "Realism in the Proletarian Novel," *Yale Review,* XVIII (December 1938), 360-374.

Strunsky, Simeon. "About Books More or Less: Said Without Flowers," *New York Times Book Review,* May 29, 1927, p. 4.

Swanberg, W. A. "Dreiser among the Slicks," *Horizon,* VII (Spring 1965), 54-61.

———. "Mencken and Dreiser," *Menckaniana*, No. 15 (Fall 1965), 6-8.

Swinnerton, Frank. "A Tribute to Theodore Dreiser," *New York Times*, December 15, 1926, p. 5.

Takashima, Atsuko. "A Study of Theodore Dreiser's Thought," *Essays and Studies in British and American Literature*, (*Ei-bei Hyoron*) VII (Summer 1959), 71-102.

Taylor, G. R. S. "Theodore Dreiser," *London Outlook*, LVIII (December 18, 1926), 607-608.

———. "The United States as Seen by an American Writer," *The Nineteenth Century*, C (December 1926), 803-815.

Taylor, Gordon O. "The Voice of Want: Frank Norris and Theodore Dreiser," *The Passages of Thought: Psychological Representation in the American Novel, 1870-1900*. New York: Oxford, 1969, pp. 136-157, 161-163.

Taylor, Walter F. "The Maturity of Naturalism: Theodore Dreiser (1871-   ) and Sherwood Anderson (1876-   )," *A History of American Letters*. Boston: American Book Co., 1936, pp. 365-380.

Thomas, J. D. "Epimetheus Bound: Theodore Dreiser and the Novel of Thought," *Southern Humanities Review*, III (Fall 1969), 346-357.

———. "The Natural Supernaturalism of Dreiser's Novels," *Rice Institute Pamphlets*, XLIV (April 1957), 112-125.

———. "The Supernatural Naturalism of Dreiser's Novels," *Rice Institute Pamphlets*, XLVI (April 1959), 53-69.

———. "Three American Tragedies: Notes on the Responsibilities of Fiction," *South Central Bulletin*, XXIV (1960), 11-15.

Thomas, Norman. "Dreiser as Economist," *Nation*, CXXXIV (April 6, 1932), 402-403.

Thompson, Alan R. "The Cult of Cruelty," *Bookman* LXXIV (January–February, 1932), 477-487.

———. "Farewell to Achilles," *Bookman*, LXX (January 1930), 465-471.

Tippetts, Sally L. "The Theatre in Dreiser's *Sister Carrie*," *Notes and Queries*, n.s. XIII (March 1966), 99-100.

Tittle, Walter. "Glimpses of Interesting Americans," *Century* CX (August 1925), 441-447.

Tjader, Marguerite. "Theodore Dreiser: World Spirit," *Free World*, XI (April 1946), 56-57.

———. "Dreiser's Last Visit to New York," *Twice-a-Year*, XIV-XV (Fall–Winter 1946–47), 217-228.

Torwill, Herbert W. "London Discusses Mr. Dreiser," *New York Times Book Review*, January 9, 1927, p. 8.

Towne, Charles H. *Adventures in Editing*. New York: Appleton, 1926, pp. 121 ff.

Trilling, Lionel. "Dreiser, Anderson, Lewis, and the Riddle of Society," *Reporter*, V (November 13, 1951), 37-40.

———. "Dreiser and the Liberal Mind," *Nation*, CLXII (April 20, 1946), 466.

———. "Reality in America," *The Liberal Imagination*. New York: Viking, 1945, pp. 3-21.

Van Doren, Carl. "American Realism," *New Republic*, XXXIV (March 21, 1923), 107-109.

———. "Contemporary American Novelists: Theodore Dreiser," *Nation*, CXLL (March 16, 1921), 400-401.

————. "*Jurgen* in Limbo," *Nation*, CXV (December 16, 1922), 613-614.

————. "The Nation and the American Novel," *Nation*, CL (February 10, 1940), 212.

————. "Theodore Dreiser," *The American Novel*, rev. ed. New York: Macmillan, 1940, pp. 245-259 ff.

————. "Theodore Dreiser," *Contemporary American Novelists, 1900–1920*. New York: Macmillan, 1928, pp. 74-83.

Van Gelder, Robert. "An Interview with Theodore Dreiser," *Writers and Writing*. New York: Scribner, 1946, pp. 164-168.

Van Vechten, Carl. "Theodore Dreiser as I Knew Him," *Yale Library Gazette*, XXV (January, 1951), 87-92.

————. "Sister Carrie's Brother," *New Republic*, CXVI (May 26, 1947), 23-5; (June 23, 1947), 24-27.

Vasil'ev, A. "Teodor Draizer," *Saint Columba and the River*. Moscow: Politizdat, 1967, pp. 45-48.

Vivas, Eliseo. "Dreiser, an Inconsistent Mechanist," *Ethics*, XLVII (July 1938), 498-508.

Von Szeliski, John J. "Dreiser's Experiment with Tragic Drama," *Twentieth Century Literature*, XII (April 1966), 31-40.

Wagenknecht, Edward. "Theodore Dreiser, The Mystic Naturalist," *Cavalcade of the American Novel*. 1954 ed. New York: Holt, 1954, pp. 281-293 ff.

Wagner, Vern. "The Maligned Style of Theodore Dreiser," *Western Humanities Review*, XIX (Spring 1965), 175-184.

Walcutt, Charles Child. "Naturalism in 1946: Dreiser and Farrell," *Accent*, VI (Summer 1946), 263-268.

———. "*Sister Carrie*: Naturalism or Novel of Manners," *Genre*, I (January 1968), 76-85.

———. "Theodore Dreiser: The Wonder and Terror of Life." *American Literary Naturalism, A Divided Stream*, Minneapolis: University of Minnesota Press, 1956, pp. 180-221.

———. "The Three States of Theodore Dreiser's Naturalism," *PMLA*, LV (March 1940), 266-289.

Waldman, Milton. "A German-American Insurgent," *Living Age*, CCCXXXI (October 1, 1926), 43-50; Reprinted from *London Mercury*, XIV (July 1926), pp. 283-291.

———. "Tendencies of the Modern Novel," *Fortnightly Review*, CXL (December 1933), 717-725.

———. "Contemporary American Authors: VII—Theodore Dreiser," *London Mercury*, XIV (July 1926), 283-291.

Walker, Charles R. "Business in the American Novel," *Bookman*, LXVI (December 1927), 401-405.

———. "How Big Is Dreiser?" *Bookman*, LXII (April 1926), 146-149.

Ward, Alfred C. *American Literature, 1880–1930*. New York: Dial, 1931, pp. 111 ff.

Warren, Robert P. "*An American Tragedy*," *Yale Review*, LII (October 1962), 1-15.

Weeks, Edward. "The Best Sellers Since 1875," *Publishers' Weekly*, CXXV (February 21, 1934), 1503-1506.

———. "A Modern Estimate of American Best Sellers, 1875-1933," *Publishers' Weekly*, CXXV (April 21, 1934), 1507.

Weimer, David R. "Heathen Catacombs," *The City as Metaphor*. New York: Random House, 1966.

Wentz, John C. "*An American Tragedy* as Epic Theater: The Piscator Dramatization," *Modern Drama*, IV (February 1962), 365-376.

West, Anthony. "Man Overboard," *New Yorker*, XXV (April 25, 1959), 169-174.

West, Ray B. *The Short Story in America, 1900–1950*. Chicago: Regnery, 1952, pp. 33-44 ff.

Westlake, Neda M. "Theodore Dreiser Collection—Addenda," *Library Chronicle* [University of Pennsylvania], XXV (Summer 1959), 55-57.

———. "Theodore Dreiser's *Notes on Life*," *Library Chronicle* [University of Pennsylvania] XX (Summer 1954), 69-75.

Whipple, T. K. "Theodore Dreiser," *Spokesmen: Modern Writers And American Life*. New York, London: Appleton, 1928, pp. 70-92.

White, William Allen. "Splitting Fiction Three Ways," in *Twelve American Novelists, The Novel of Tomorrow*. Indianapolis: Bobbs-Merrill, 1922, pp. 123-133.

Willen, Gerald. "Dreiser's Moral Seriousness," *University of Kansas City Review*, XXIII (Spring 1957), 181-187.

Williams, Philip. "The Chapter Titles of *Sister Carrie*," *American Literature*, XXXVI (November 1964), 359-365.

Wilson, Edmund. "Equity for Americans," *New Republic*, LXX (March 30, 1932).

Wilson, James S. "The Changing Novel," *Virginia Quarterly Review*, X (January 1934), 42-52.

Wilson, William E. "*The Titan* and the Gentlemen," *Antioch Review*, XXIII (Spring 1963), 25-34.

Witham, W. Tasker, *Panorama of American Literature*. New York: Stephen Daye, 1947, pp. 219-223 ff.

Wollstein, R. H. "You Know Mr .Dreiser; The American Tragedian Turns His Freudian Eyes on Music," *Musical America*, XLIX (February 25, 1929), 35-7, 55-56.

Wolfe, Don M. "Theodore Dreiser and the Human Enigma," *The Image of Man in America*. Dallas: Southern Methodist University Press, 1957, pp. 317-337.

Woollcott, Alexander. "An American Tragedy," in Moses, Montrose J. and John Mason Brown, eds. *The American Theater As Seen By Its Critic, 1752-1934*. New York: Cooper Square, 1967, pp. 247-249.

Wycherley, H. Allen. "Mechanism and Vitalism in Dreiser's Non-fiction," *Texas Studies in Literature and Language*, XI (1969), 1039-1049.

Yamamoto, Shuji. "Religion of Dreiser: Its Four Aspects," *Kyushu American Literature*, X (1967), 70-74.

Ziff, Larzer. "A Decade's Delay: Theodore Dreiser," *The American 1890's*. New York: Viking, 1966, pp. 339-348.

Selected Reviews of Dreiser's Major Works

A more complete list can be found in Kazin and Shapiro, *The Stature of Theodore Dreiser*.

An American Tragedy (1925).

Sherman, Stuart. *Books, New York Herald and Tribune*, January 3, 1926, p. 1.

Anderson, Sherwood. *Saturday Review of Literature*, II (January 9, 1926), 475.

Edgett, E. F. *Boston Transcript*, January 9, 1926, p. 3.

Duffus, R. L. *New York Times Book Review*, January 10, 1926, p. 1.

Darrow, Clarence. *Literary Review, New York Evening Post*, January 16, 1926, p. 1.

Tully, Jim. *International Book Review*, February 1926, p. 167.

Krutch, J. W. *Nation*, CXXII (February 10, 1926), 152.

Anon. *Saturday Review of Literature*, II (February 20, 1926), 569.

Whipple, T. K. *New Republic*, XLVI (March 17, 1926), 113.

Powys, C. *Dial*, LXXX (April 1926), 331.

Muir, Edwin. *Nation and Athenaeum*, XL (October 16, 1926), 88.

The Best Short Stories of Theodore Dreiser (1947).

Anon. *New Yorker*, XXIII (March 29, 1947), 110.

Anon. *Time*, XLIX (April 7, 1947), 114.

A Book About Myself (1922).

Anon. *New York Time Book Review*, December 24, 1922, p. 14.

Edgett, E. F. *Boston Transcript*, December 30, 1922, p. 4.

Rascoe, Burton. *New York Tribune*, December 31, 1922, p. 17.

Krutch, J. W. *Literary Review, New York Evening Post*, January 20, 1923, p. 396.

The Bulwark (1946).

Spiller, R. E. *Saturday Review of Literature*, XXIX (March 23, 1946), 23.

Wilson, Edmund. *New Yorker*, XXII (March 23, 1946), 88.

Flanagan, J. T. *Book Week, The Chicago Sun*, March 24, 1946, p. 2.

Gregory, Horace. *Weekly Book Review, New York Herald Tribune*, March 24, 1946, p. 1.

Matthiessen, F. O. *New York Times Book Review*, March 24, 1946, p. 1.

Trilling, Diana. *Nation*, CLXII (April 20, 1946), 466.

Prescott, Orville, *Yale Review*, XXXV (Summer 1946), 767.

Chains (1927).

Stuart, L. *New York Times Book Review*, May 15, 1927, p. 2.

Van Doren, Carl. *Books, New York Herald Tribune*, May 22, 1927, p. 3.

Anon. *Boston Transcript*, June 11, 1927, p. 2.

Munson, G. B. *Saturday Review of Literature*, III (June 25, 1927), 928.

The Color of a Great City (1923).

Anon. *New York Times Book Review*, December 23, 1923, p. 7.

Anon. *Boston Transcript*, January 9, 1924, p. 4.

Dawn (1931).

Britten, F. H. *Books, New York Herald Tribune*, May 10, 1931, p. 5.

Jack, P. M. *New York Times Book Review*, May 10, 1931, p. 5.

Hazlitt, Henry. *Nation*, CXXXII (June 3, 1931), 613.

Herick, Robert. *Saturday Review of Literature*, VII (June 6, 1931), 875.

Thompson, A. R. *Bookman*, LXXIII (July 1931), 583.

Anon. *Times Literary Supplement*, July 23, 1931, p. 575.

Arvin, Newton. *New Republic*, LXVII (August 5, 1931), 319.

Burdett, Osbert. *Saturday Review*, CLII (August 8, 1931), 186.

Dreiser Looks at Russia (1928).

Anon. *Books, New York Herald Tribune*, December 23, 1928, p. 3.

Shanks, E. *Saturday Review*, CXLVII (May 11, 1929), 644.

Anon. *Times Literary Supplement*, June 27, 1929, p. 501.

The Financier (1912).

Mencken, H. L. *New York Times Book Review*, November 10, 1912, p. 654.

Free (1918).

Edgett, E. F. *Boston Transcript*, August 28, 1918, p. 6.
Anon. *Dial*, LXV (December 28, 1918), 630.

A Gallery of Women (1929).

Hansen, Harry. *New York World*, November 30, 1929, p. 13.

Anon. *New York Times Book Review*, December 1, 1929, p. 2.

Hobson, Thayer. *Books, New York Herald Tribune*, December 1, 1929, p. 5.

Porterfield, A. W. *Outlook*, CLIII (December 18, 1929), 628.

Brown, R. A. *Saturday Review of Literature*, VI (February 8, 1930), 707.

The "Genius" (1915).

    Edgett, E. F. *Boston Transcript*, October 9, 1915, p. 9.

    Anon. *New York Times Book Review*, October 10, 1915, p. 362.

    Anon. *Nation*, CI (October 14, 1915), 461.

    Hale, E. *Dial*, LIX (November 11, 1915), 422.

    Bourne Randolph. *New Republic*, V (November 20, 1915), Supplement, p. 5.

The Hand of the Potter (1918).

    Anon. *Nation*, CIX (September 6, 1919), 340.

    Anon. *Boston Transcript*, September 17, 1919, p. 4.

    Bennett, J. L. *New Republic*, XX (October 8, 1919), p. 297.

    Anon. *New York Times Book Review*, October 26, 1919, p. 598.

Hey Rub-A-Dub (1920).

    Anon. *New York Times Book Review*, October 26, 1919, p. 598.

    Brooks, Van Wyck. *Nation*, CX (May 1, 1920), 595.

    Anon. *New Republic*, XXII (May 26, 1920), 423.

A Hoosier Holiday (1916).

    Edgett, E. F. *Boston Transcript*, November 15, 1916, p. 8.

    Anon. *Dial*, LXI (November 30, 1916), 474.

Jennie Gerhardt (1911).

 Anon. *New York Times Book Review*, November 19, 1911, p. 728.

 Winter, Calvin. *Bookman* XXXIV (December, 1911), 432.

 Anon. *Independent*, LXXI (December 7, 1911), 1267.

Moods Philosophic and Emotional Cadenced and Declaimed (1935).

 Walton, E. L. *Books, New York Herald Tribune*, June 23, 1935, p. 4.

 Benet, W. R. *Saturday Review of Literature*, XXII (June 29, 1935), 18.

 Hutchison, Percy. *New York Times Book Review*, July 7, 1935, p. 10.

Plays of the Natural and Supernatural (1916).

 Anon. *Boston Transcript*, March 18, 1916, p. 9.

Sister Carrie (1900).

 Cooper, Frederic T. *Bookman*, XXV (May 1907), 287.
 ———. *Forum*, XXXIX (July 1907), 117.

 Rhodes, Harrison. *Bookman*, XXV (May 1907), 298.

 Anon. *New York Times Book Review*, May 25, 1907, p. 332.

 Coates, Joseph H. *North American Review*, CLXXXVI (October 1907), 288.

The Stoic, Doubleday (1947).

> Cowley, Malcolm. *New York Times Book Review*, November 23, 1947, p. 7.
>
> Conroy, Jack *Chicago Sun Book Week*, December 3, 1947, p. 4A.
>
> Lydenberg, John. *Saturday Review of Literature*, XXX (December 6, 1947), 36.
>
> Anon. *New York Herald Tribune Weekly Book Review*, December 7, 1947, p. 54.

The Titan (1914).

> Edgett, E. F. *Boston Transcript*, May 23, 1914, p. 8.
>
> Hawthorne, H. *New York Times Book Review*, May 24, 1914, p. 241.
>
> Cary, Lucian. *Dial*, LVI (June 16, 1911), p. 504.
>
> Anon. *Atlantic Monthly*, CXIV (October 1914), 523.

Tragic America (1932).

> Chase, Stuart. *Books, New York Herald Tribune* January 24, 1932, p. 2.
>
> Strunsky, Simeon. *New York Times Book Review*, January 24, 1932, p. 10.
>
> Jones, Eliot. *Saturday Review of Literature*, VIII (February 27, 1932), 555.
>
> Wilson, Edmund. *New Republic*, LXX (March 30, 1932) 185.
>
> Thomas, Norman. *Nation*, CXXXIV (April 6, 1932), 402.

Anon. *Times Literary Supplment*, August 4, 1932, p. 550.

Agar, Herbert. *New Statesman and Nation*, IV (August 6, 1932), 160.

A Traveler At Forty (1913).

Edgett, E. F. *Boston Transcript*, December 3, 1913, p. 4.

Twelve Men (1919).

Edgett, E. F. *Boston Transcript*, April 30, 1919, p. 6.

Anon. *New Republic*, XIX (May 3, 1919), 30.

Anon. *Nation*, CVIII (May 24, 1919), 838.

Anon. *Times Literary Supplement*, August 21, 1919, p. 446.